GOING SOLO

100 ORIGINAL AUDITION MONOLOGUES

by JASON MILLIGAN

SAMUEL FRENCH, INC.

45 West 25th Street   NEW YORK 10010
7623 Sunset Boulevard   HOLLYWOOD 90046
LONDON   TORONTO

For Stefanie ...

IMPORTANT BILLING AND CREDIT
REQUIREMENTS

All producers of GOING SOLO *must* give credit to the Author of the Monologues in all programs distributed in connection with performances of the Monologues and in all instances in which the title of the Monologues appears for purposes of advertising, publicizing or otherwise exploiting the Monologues and/or a production. The name of the Author *must* also appear on a separate line, on which no other name appears, immediately following the title, and *must* appear in size of type not less than fifty percent the size of the title type.

FOREWORD

In 1986 my friend Robert Spera, a wonderful director and acting teacher, came to me with an idea: he suggested we write a collection of original audition monologues for actors. Rob and I had both worked as actors and we knew all too well how difficult it was to find pieces in existing plays that jumped off the page and worked in an audition situation. With the help of Deborah Cowles Scott, we set to work to create such a book. Published by Samuel French in 1987, it was called *Actors Write for Actors* and the three of us followed it up in 1989 with a second collection, *Encore!*

In this volume are 100 new audition pieces: 50 for men and 50 for women. I have concentrated on creating many different character types and many different situations in these monologues—both funny and dramatic. However, let me say that the actor may find pieces in the "women" section which might work for him and the actress may find something in the "men" section which works for her. If so, use it. The whole idea behind this collection is to give you a toolbox, which will hopefully help get you a job. Whether you're auditioning for producers, directors, acting teachers, whatever the situation—there's a piece in here, *somewhere,* that's right for you and for the occasion.

I'd like to relay my thanks to Debbie and Rob for teaching me so much about writing for the audition situation and I am pleased to be *Going Solo* with this new book.

Break a leg!

Jason Milligan
New York
June 1992

CONTENTS

MEN

WOMEN

AM I NEXT?
BETSY BOOKWORM
BORIS
COUGH DROPS
DETAILS
DIRTY LOOKS
DO NO WRONG
EYE TO EYE
FAITH
FAKE PLANTS
FIND YOURSELF
FIRE WITH FIRE
FIRST STEP
FLATTERY WILL GET YOU
  KILLED
FOOD FIGHT
FRESH MEAT
HIDDEN
HOPE
HUMAN ICICLES
I LOVE ANIMALS
I'M NOT STUPID
LOSS
MAKING IT
MAN IN THE SHOEBOX
ME IN A NUTSHELL

MEDICINE
NEVER LOOK BACK
NEW YEAR'S DAY
NEW PERSPECTIVE
NICE LITTLE TOUCHES
NO THREAT
OBJECT
PEOPLE LIKE YOU
PERFECT FANTASY MAN
PRIDE
READY TO ACT
SELF-ESTEEM
SEX APPEAL
SKI MASKS
SLAVE TO SICKNESS
SPONTANEITY
STATE OF MIND
STRENGTH
SWIMMING WITH SHARKS
THE $10,000 WOMAN
TWO-FACED
UH-HUH
WALKING COOKBOOK
WELL INFORMED
WHAT IF

MEN

AMATEUR NIGHT

What are we going to *tell* him? What do you *think* we're going to tell him? We are going to look him straight in the eye and we are going to LIE THROUGH OUR TEETH, Janice. That's right. I know, I know, you've got such a *penchant* for "telling it like it is," but *this* time, you just can't. You cannot. Look at me. THERE IS NO WAY WE ARE GOING TO TELL HIM THE TRUTH. Because! He's been going down there every Monday night for the last six months for Amateur Night, getting up at that microphone, and wailing out these horrible songs of his. I mean, my God. Does anyone *really* want to hear eight and a half minutes of "Pinocchio's Bride"? Where the hell did he even get the *idea* to write a song called "Pinocchio's Bride"? I mean, did you *hear* the lyrics? It's SO SICK! Maybe it would've been bearable if his guitar had been in tune. But it was horrible! It was totally humiliating to see him up there, knowing that he does it, week after week after week, hoping to get "discovered." This is his *dream*, Janice. He is *living out his dream*. And if we tell him the truth ... pffft! There goes the dream. It's over. (*Beat.*) We can't pull the rug out from under him. This is *one* instance where you are just going to have to grit your teeth and tell him you thought it was—(*Pause as HE searches for the "perfect word"—but HE can't seem to find it ... Looks to "Janice" for help in finding the right word. In silence HE gropes for it, can't find it. HE just shrugs.*)

11

ANGELS

Food? (*Bitter laugh.*) Food didn't *matter*. I didn't care about *food*.
Food was just ... something I hadda have to keep me goin'. I was
eatin' cat food right outta the can, baby. With my *fingers*. It didn't
matter! All I was living for was one more fix. You hear what I'm
sayin'? (*Beat.*) Here. (*Pulls his sleeves up, shows his wrists.*) You
see that? I didn't know which way to cut. *Now* I know that you cut
this way ... (*Parallel to veins.*) instead of *that* way. (*Across the
wrist.*) But at the time, hell, I didn't know how to kill myself. I was
just some poor dumb bastard from Brooklyn who couldn't pay for
his drug habit. I was gonna try sleeping pills, but I remember I
didn't have enough money to buy 'em. So I cut my wrists with a
cat food can lid and I laid on the bathroom floor of a welfare hotel
bleeding for two days. Only reason they found me was somebody
hadda take a crap so bad they finally complained. See, bathroom's
down the hall in one a them places. You share the bathroom with
six, seven other people. Super broke the door down and found me.
When he busted in, I didn't know what the hell was goin' on. I
thought, like, he was some kinda Angel and I had died and gone to
Heaven. But then, a few days later, I woke up in rehab strapped to a
bed and, man, *that* time I thought I had died and gone to *hell*! (*Beat.*)
I couldn't figure out *why* I was given another fuckin' chance. I
mean, look at me! Why the hell was *I* spared? But now I know.
(*Beat.*) You got a choice, baby. Which way do you wanna go?
(*Holds up his wrists.*) *Don't*. You got a lot goin' for you, and it's
just ... *stupid*, to end up like I did.

BAD INFLUENCE

My dad was always pretty strict with me, too. I thought he was a real son of a bitch, but you have to remember that *my* dad was a Baptist minister in a small Alabama town and under his roof, there wasn't a whole lot of room for ... well, *fun.* We didn't ever do *anything* fun. We didn't have a record player—this was back when people *had* record players; or a TV; we didn't *ever* go to the movies or to parties; we weren't allowed to *dance* ... in short, growing up pretty much *sucked.* You've got it made in comparison with— c'mon, now, just sit there and listen to this, okay? I'm trying to *tell* you something! (*Beat.*) When I got older, I realized that my dad had just been doing what he thought was right. Maybe he was a little misguided; maybe not. Who can say? But when I was a kid, I couldn't see that. All I knew when I was your age was that I was mad as hell and I wasn't going to listen to him. Just like you're doing to me, now. (*Beat.*) Chris, I don't think you oughtta be hanging around with Tom and Greg so much, because I think they're a bad influence. I know, I *know* they're your friends. I know that. But you gotta look at it: they're *always* in trouble! Chris, they got *arrested.* All three of you were together and you're lucky you didn't get picked up too. *Shoplifting?* (*Beat.*) I know. I know I'm not your father. But I am your legal guardian. Your mom and dad decided that *I'm* the one they wanted to look after you if anything ever happened to them. I have tried really hard never to sit here and tell you what to do ... but I really think this is what they would want. I really do. I just hope ... you'll try and see that.

13

BALD MEN

What am I doing? What does it *look* like I'm doing? That's my suitcase; I'm packing—And when I'm done packing I'm gonna carry the suitcase out to the car and I'm gonna start the car and I'm gonna drive away. Far away. Hand me those socks, will you? I've got to get a move on before it gets dark. *Why?* What do you mean, "why?" Because! In the next five to ten years, I am going to be *bald!* (*Beat.*) Oh, right. That's right. Go ahead and laugh at me! But I *know* how you feel about bald men, Katie. I can't *help* but know! Every time we pass a bald guy on the street, you giggle. That really irritating high-pitched giggle of yours. (*HE imitates it.*) On TV, in the movies, a bald crown pops up and you just go crazy! Laughing like a hyena! (*Imitates this sound as well.*) I think it is sick and I think you have some kind of chemical imbalance or something. To laugh at people like that. But never mind what I think. Let's talk about what you think about *me*. Oh, right. Right. You love me. Yeah. *Now*. But what happens in six years when my manhood is washing down the drain? My hair. I'm talking about my *hair*. When we first met, you told me one of the things you found most attractive about me was my locks! Well, they're goin', sweetheart! I just found out today that my *grandfather* was bald! Just like my dad! And if you put any stock in heredity ... well, you just figure it out: (*Holds his hair back with his hand to "appear" bald.*) It's not a pretty sight, is it? Oh, go on! Laugh. But by this time tomorrow I'll be crossing the state line. By this time—What? You what? That is the most ridiculous ... You think Telly Savalas is *sexy*? (*Beat.*) Well, then that changes things, doesn't it? That means ... (*Beat.*) That means there's hope for me yet!

14

BILLY SCOTT

Billy Scott ... As long as I live, I will never forget Billy Scott. Billy Scott was a senior back when I was a sophomore. He was on the football team and the baseball team. And, if I remember correctly, he was also on the wrestling team. He wore a letter jacket everywhere he went. And, worst of all, he *looked perfect!* Perfect! Like a friggin' movie star! Every guy at Randolph High wanted to *be* Billy Scott. Every girl wanted to go *out* with Billy Scott. And me ... I hated Billy Scott. Hated him because of what he put us through. He was the perfect role model. And all of the rest of us were expected to live up to what he was. But one day ... I found out that Billy Scott was a big fake. And that's when I *really* started to hate him. See, my dad used to make me wax his car. Every Saturday afternoon, I'm all set to go out and mess around with the guys but *no*. I have to wax Dad's car first. He had this big black Cadillac, it took *forever* to wax. Have you ever waxed a black car before? No matter how hard you try to buff it, a black car always looks smudgy. But not Billy Scott's car. It *never* looked smudgy! He had a shiny black car and it never looked smudgy. And my dad pointed this out to me over and over and over again. Well ... one day I happened to walk by Billy Scott's house and I learned a big lesson: Billy Scott didn't wax his car. He made a couple of freshmen do it. I talked to them. He made them do his homework for him too. And if the car didn't look perfect, if the homework wasn't right ... he'd beat the crap out of these little guys! That's how I first learned about power, avarice and deceit. From Billy Scott. But nature always provides the last laugh. Everything all evens out in the end. Last time I saw Billy Scott, he was two hundred pounds, bald, wearing a leisure suit, and driving a delivery truck for the local appliance store. I know it doesn't look like there's justice in the world, but trust me. Things have a way of working out.

BLOOD

I always thought, blood was thicker than a man's greed. That's what I *thought*, y'see. But ... I's wrong. My own brother stole ever'thing I owned from me. Ever'thing. On account a I couldn't read or write no ways. I was ill—ill—(*Beat.*) *You* know what I'm tryin' to say ... But I'm better now. I can sign my own name. Lemme show you. You want me to show you? I'll show you. Here. See this piece a paper? (*Signs his name on a piece of paper, very, very slowly.*) It takes me awhile ... took me a whole entire summer to *learn* ... on account a I never had no schoolin'. There. (*HE's finished with the signature.*) My brother, Daddy sent him off to that school. Learnt all these *things* ... he could tell you how much money was in yo' *sock*. How many jelly beans was in a canning jar. Yeah, he learnt a lot ... (*Beat.*) Daddy left him and me a hunnerd acres apiece, see. An' Bayliss—he's my brother—he made me sign these three pieces a paper. I put a "X" on 'em, on account a that was back before I knew how to sign my name. Man from the courthouse told me one day, said my hunnerd acres ain't *mine* no more. I says yes they is. He says no, you put your "X" on Bayliss' three pieces a paper. Now they's his. That's what made me wisht I could learn how to sign my name, read and write. Little gal over to the elementary school taught me. (*Beat.*) It's a shame, really. That a man's brother could *do* that to him. I thought blood was thicker'n that. (*Beat.*) I guess I was wrong.

BOILED EGGS

I will *never* look at women as objects again. I just won't. I learned my lesson. For years, all I looked for was a pretty face, or nice legs, or—you know. But not anymore. I wanna tell you a little story, Charlie. About a little ... experience I had a couple of years ago. One morning, on the way to work, I saw what, up to that moment in my life, was the most spectacular woman I had ever laid eyes on! We're sitting right across from each other on the R Train and boy, let me tell you. She was something. Strawberry blonde hair. About five-six. Legs up to here. *Incredible*! So here I am, I'm on the way to work, and the train stops at 34th Street. She gets up to get off. Now, as you know, I'm supposed to go on to 8th Street—but this time, I *can't*! It's like there's some kinda spell on me. I'm *drawn* to her! I'm captivated by her. So I decide to follow her ... I figure, okay, so I'll be *late* today. I *gotta* see where she goes. So ... we go up the subway stairs and I'm right behind her. God, could she move. But, just as she reaches the top of the steps, she drops something. Smack. It hits the concrete. Her Ten-Pack. But, of course there I am, I don't miss a beat, I scoop it up and hand it to her and as I do, she turns to look at me. I see her face up close for the first time— the most beautiful deep blue eyes I have ever seen. I'm speechless. I don't know what to say, but I'm *saved* because she is the first one to speak and as she opens her mouth ... I see that she's got *food* crammed all in between each and every one of her teeth! BOILED EGGS! Chewed-up, undigested egg whites caked all in her mouth! It was disgusting! Five minutes before, I woulda given my left arm just to kiss her, and now all I could think was—BOILED EGGS! (*HE shudders.*) I'm just telling you this to try and help you, Charlie. Take it from me. Don't put too much stock into appearances. 'Cause if you put all your money on appearances ... you may end up with BOILED EGGS.

17

BREADWINNER

I made a pact with myself. I made a pact, see. I told myself that they would never go without. That Maggie and the kids, they'd never go without. This was something I *swore* to myself, a long time ago ... and I have kept that promise. Steel mill shut down, I was outta work for thirteen months. But they did *not* go hungry. I did odd jobs to keep food on the table. Coats on their backs. I fixed your plumbing half a dozen times. Never overcharged you. Well ... you know as well as I do, it hasn't been easy. Hell, nothing's "easy." There've been times I've had to resort to things—well, things you wouldn't approve of. But you're sure as hell the one to call somebody "unethical." Is that a word you'd use? Or would you say "dishonest?" "Cheat?" "Thief?" "Liar?" (*Beat.*) Yes, Arlin. I took the money. And I'd do it again if I had to. I mean it. I'm not ashamed and I'm not gonna apologize. You're so damn rich you wouldn't a missed it anyway. But your pride says you got to do something about it. Your pride says you got to swat me down like a fly. So go ahead. Fire me, if that's what you want to do. What you "have" to do. I already did what *I* had to do. (*Beat.*) Like I said ... I made a pact, Arlin. And I can't break it, no matter what.

BROTHERS

What is this chicken-shit attitude all of a sudden? Huh? You're such
a fuckin' baby, Tony. My little baby brother, you're such a fuckin'
cry baby. It's not like we killed some guy or anything. Everybody,
Tony, *every*body does stuff like this. Stuff worse than us. A *lot*
worse than us. We're not the only ones trying to improve our lot in
life. And who did we hurt, huh? Did we sell crack to a nine-year-old
girl and fry her brains? No. Did we rape an old lady? No. Nothing
like that, we didn't do nothing like that. All we did was *borrow* a
few credit card numbers. I mean, what's so bad about that? These
people, they dispute the charges, they don't even hafta pay for it.
And who gets hurt? Huh? I'll tell you who gets hurt: Nobody.
Aahh, Jesus! Don't start with all that "conscience" shit again. You
got a conscience? Go watch MARY POPPINS, but don't tell me
about it. Listen: You got a *car* now. You wanted a car. We *got* you
that Cadillac. Like, American Express can't afford to buy you a
Cadillac? I got news for you, Tony: They ain't *hurtin'*! (*Beat.*)
What? You—*what*? You can't take it back! Tony—listen to me—
will you—LISTEN! You *can't take the car back*! It's *yours* now! So
get your ass out there and drive it, will ya? It's been sittin' in my
carport all day long. Pop? What about Pop? (*Beat.*) *Moral*? Pop?
Hah. What, you think Pop never did anything "indecent" his whole
life? I got news for you, Anthony: Pop was no saint. Pop used to
do a lotta stuff that'd make your hair curl. He used to run numbers
for those guys out in Brooklyn. Yeah. When he was your age. Well,
he did a lot worse'n that. But you're not old enough to hear the rest
of it. Yeah, well, when you turn twenty-one, I'll tell you
everything. (*Beat.*) Well, then. Now you know. So take the car,
willya? Okay? Will you take the car? At least say you'll sleep on it,
eh? Good. I *need* a brother I can depend on. Capisce?

DOPPLER EFFECT

Man, you've gotta get ahold of yourself. Before you go in there.
Because I'm tellin' you. Everything you do, everything you *say* ...
it has its effect. You may not think so, but it does. Somewhere
down the line. I'm not saying, "Don't be honest with your
feelings." But let's just forget that therapy crap, okay? It's
horseshit. Just toss it out the window, because *each* of your
actions—it's like the Doppler Effect. Remember back in high
school? Mr. Henry's science class. Remember when he did that
thing where he dropped a rock in the water and the waves moved
out, away from where the rock hit, in wider and wider circles? Yeah,
the Doppler Effect. Yeah, well, eventually those waves *touch*
something. Something floating on the water ... the shore.
Something is touched by the splash that started those waves. Let's
say I'm pissed off about something and I come in here and yell at
you. And you get pissed off and you go home and take it out on
your wife. And things get real thick in your house and your son
starts acting up and your wife punishes him really severely because
she's mad at you 'cause you were mad at me 'cause I was mad about
some other bullshit that didn't have anything to *do* with you! Don't
you see? You're a teacher, Eddie. A fuckin' *teacher*. And if you go
in there and take it out on those kids ... it's like a chain reaction. It
affects people all the way down the line—and who *knows* where and
how? (*Beat.*) Look. I know you're pissed right now. Fine.
Somebody dumped on you, and if I was you, I'd be pissed too. But
don't you dare take it out on those kids. Cause you don't know how
far those waves are gonna *reach.*

EMOTIONAL

It's not *that* bad. (*Beat.*) Look, don't make such a big *deal* out of it, okay? *Please.* I'm begging you—no. No. No, don't. Don't—Oh my God! Cheryl! You're doing it again. Yes you are. You're *crying!* (*It has obviously gotten "worse."*) Oh, no, no. God help me ... *(Looks around, embarrassed.)* Every time. Every time we go out. You *cry.* You *wail.* The soup is too hot. A bum looks in the window. The waiter stumps his toe—anything sets you off! (*Apparently, a wail comes out.*) Shhh! Shhhh! Honey, please! I'm sorry. I just—Look. I want to talk about this, but you can't keep wailing the whole time. Okay? You've got to try and *listen.* Honey? Good. That's good. Better. (*Beat.*) Now you *know* I love you—your mascara's running; yeah, there—but this whole thing with the tear ducts is driving me up the wall! At first, you know, I thought it was *cute.* How *emotional* you were. And it *was* cute. But honey. Enough's enough. I—now, now *listen* to me. Last night I got *one hour* of sleep. You *cried* until four o'clock in the morning because the *NIGHT LIGHT* BURNED OUT! CHERYL! HAVE YOU LOST YOUR MIND? YOU HAVE GOT TO GET AHOLD OF YOURSELF BECAUSE THIS IS A VERY SERIOUS PROBLEM AND WE CAN'T SOLVE IT UNLESS—(*SHE obviously starts crying again:*) Oh, Cheryl ... no. No. Okay. Go on. *Cry* ... (*Beat.*) But I'm warning you: I'm running out of Kleenex! (*Whips a tissue out of his pocket and holds it out, offering it to her.*)

FLAVOR OF THE MONTH

Don't let it go to your head. No, no, you did a great job, I'm not saying that. It's a great campaign. I wish *I'd* come up with it. But you gotta remember, this is advertising, and advertising is a *business*. Right now you think you can get away with anything. Right now you think you can do no wrong. They're infatuated with you. So infatuated that if you were to take a shit right on the boardroom table, they'd stand there in awe of it. Look, don't you be a smartass with me! I know what I'm talking about! And don't tell me I'm washed up either. I AM NOT WASHED UP! *(Beat.)* Well. Maybe I am ... *(Beat.)* I remember when I first came here. I was Flavor of the Month, just like you. They loved me. They loved all of my ideas. Whatever I came up with, they worshipped it. Just like you. I got to where I thought I could come up with this stuff in my sleep. And I could, too, no matter how wild my ideas were, no matter how far out, no matter how outta left field, they went for 'em. Loved 'em. Loved *me*! But then ... *another* new guy came along. And all of a sudden I was yesterday's news. They started going to *him* first, instead of me. They started taking *him* to lunch, instead of me. What can I say? That's how it happens. *(Beat.)* So don't go getting too full of yourself, pal. Not just yet. Yeah, yeah, you're King Shit right now, but I gotta *tell* ya ... it doesn't last.

GIRL TROUBLE

I don't want this to sound all ... *macho* or anything, but I've always had a way with girls. You know. Always known what to say, how to say it, what to do. It's just come ... natural to me. A lotta guys bitch and moan all the time and tell me they don't even know how to say *hi* to a girl—but me? I've *never* had that problem. (*Beat.*) Until now: Eileen. *You* saw her last night. Beautiful, huh? Offhand, I'd say the most beautiful girl I've ever known. When she walked into my life, I couldn't believe my luck. I thought, this is too good to be *true*! But there's this ... *problem*, see, and I don't know how to point it out to her. Well ... it's like this. (*Beat.*) She picks her nose. No, now, I'm serious. She is perfection defined in the human form and she's the most graceful creature God ever put on this earth but she seems to have this deep-seated need to ... prod around in her nasal cavity with her index finger. We're in a restaurant, the movies, some public place where there's lots of people around; they're all *admiring* her and all of a sudden, there she goes, digging around in there like some big burly guy. Last night in the bar I overheard this fella whisper to his date, "what a shame" when Eileen started going at it. I *know* I ougtta say something to her, I know I've *got* to ... but I don't know *what*. And the weirdest thing of all is, even though everybody who ever sees this is just really grossed-out by it and everything? (*Beat.*) I kinda *like* it. Because ... well, she is the most perfect woman I've ever known—physically—and this just sorta makes her ... I don't know how to say it ... just sorta makes her more ... *real*. (*Beat.*) What can I say? It *must* be true love.

GROWING UP

Where's my lamp? I liked that lamp. I made that lamp in Shop, remember? I know it kind of electrocuted you whenever you cut it on ... but I liked it. And that bookshelf. Where's that bookshelf I made? You know the one, it had the shelves all going at a thirty-degree angle ... it was practically useless, but I liked it. What'd you do with all that stuff? (*Beat.*) You threw it *out*? You mean, out in the *trash*? Like old cat food cans or something? God, Mother! That was all part of my *life*! I can't believe you just tossed it! No, I didn't. I didn't! I *never* thought of this place as a storage shed, Mother, I always I thought of this place as home. And when you come home, you're supposed to be surrounded by all the things, the things that—(*Beat.*) Well, maybe you're right. Maybe it was cluttering up the place. But ... my old room doesn't feel like my old room anymore. Every time I cut that lamp on and got that little shock ... I felt good. It sort of reminded me of when I was little. When I was taken care of and protected from things and ... oh, well. No use crying over spilt milk, eh? No use crying about growing up. We all gotta grow up sometime, right? (*Beat.*) I'm sorry. Here I am, getting all bent out of shape cause you threw out all that old crap ... At least you saved the *room*. I guess I oughta stop complaining and just be grateful for *that*, huh? (*Beat.*) Thanks, Mom.

HAIR

My hair is growing at a furious pace. Yeah, well, that may not sound like a big deal to *you*, but for me, it's an *enormous* problem. ENORMOUS! (*Beat.*) No, you don't understand. It *won't stop*! IT WON'T STOP! And do you know why? Do you have any *idea*? (*HE suddenly feels a headache coming on and massages his temples.*) Stress. It's a direct result of stress on me in my everyday life. Things that are just *so easy* for other people—taking the bus, asking someone next to you in a diner to pass you the ketchup, buying a pack of rubbers—make me so uptight! Look at it. I'm sure it's a coupla inches longer since we sat down. See, when I was a kid, Mom and Pop'd get me a crew cut—remember those?—on Memorial Day and that'd last me all summer long. Why, you ask? I'll tell you why: because when you're a kid, you don't have any PROBLEMS! But *now*—God, my hair just grows and grows in proportion to all the problems I have and yesterday when I looked, it was down to my BUTT! I hadda get it cut on the way over here, you just don't know how humiliating it is! My girlfriend—*ex*-girlfriend, I should say, but that's a whole 'nother story—she nicknamed me Rapunzel. Can you believe it? RAPUNZEL! Well, I can't deal with it anymore. I can't. I just can't. That's why I came to you, Leon. I need a little favor. (*Beat.*) I want you to blow my brains out. See? I bought this gun at a pawn shop. I've cleaned it and oiled it and it's all ready to go, all you gotta do is, you know. Flick your finger. And then my constant curtain of stress will at last be LIFTED ... and my hair will cease once again to grow. Will you do that for me, Leon? (*Beat.*) Leon?

I NEED MEAT

I know a guy who ate a *cat* once. Isn't that *sick*? Oh, yeah. He
actually skinned it, cooked it, fried it, and ate it. (*Beat.*) I dunno.
Probably pretty awful, I would think. *He* liked it. At least, that's
what he *said* ... (*Beat.*) I know, I wouldn't want to either. And I
wouldn't expect *you* to, either. I wouldn't. If I decided—and don't
worry, I won't—if I decided that I wanted a heaping platter of—fresh
Chihuahua, say—I wouldn't force *you* to eat it *too*! (*Beat.*) Well,
Diane. That's what I'm saying. This vegetarian thing of yours ...
it's kinda ... *getting* to me. I mean, you're your own person. You
wanna eat *dog* shit, that's fine with me. And I'm glad you enjoy
being a Veggie, I really and truly am. I think it's wonderful. You
seem much happier, much skinnier, and much more ... energetic.
But it's starting to take its toll on me. Bean sprouts and I just do
not mix. Tofu and I ... are not best friends. Diane. I have had the
runs for *two weeks*! I haven't been able to bench press one-eighty
since you made me go Veggie! I don't have the strength anymore,
the *endurance* I used to have. I fall asleep at work. It's awful! I
NEED MEAT! I'm sorry! I'm sorry, but I DO! I've been trying to
sneak steaks on the sly! I've been stopping off at Louie's Bar on the
way home every day and having him cook me a ribeye! IT'S
AWFUL! I FEEL LIKE I'M BEING UNFAITHFUL! I can't do it
anymore, and you gotta let me go from the Veggie Grasp! You're
never gonna convert me, I swear, IF I PUT ONE MORE BITE OF
WHEAT GERM IN MY MOUTH—! (*Beat; HE holds back a gag,
then:*) I'm sorry, Diane. I really am sorry. I didn't mean to shout. I
just—I *knew* that, sooner or later, you'd smell the steak sauce on
my breath ... and I didn't want to get caught in a *lie*.

IMPOSTER

Do me a favor. Would you try not to look too good out there? Just—you know. Maybe you could look kinda like you don't know what you're doing. For me. Why? 'Cause I'm *scared!* I work with all these people every day of the week and to have to get out here and play *softball* with them? Why? Why do we have to go through these rituals? God, you're lucky, Annette. I mean, your dad played ball with you when you were growing up. Not me. Mine was always ... off rebuilding an engine or watching Roller Derby or out drinking with his buddies. I never learned all these "guy" things! I never *learned* how to catch a fly ball without cringing like a fool, or how to tackle somebody without breaking my kneecaps or how to dribble and walk at the same time ... you take it for granted 'cause you know how to do all these things. But me. I've weaseled out of basketball games and touch football games and every kind of game you can think of, but they wouldn't let me get out of the "Employees and Spouses Softball Weekend." These people think I'm an athlete 'cause I got a decent build and they're *counting* on me to win this game! Can you believe it? They've been fighting for weeks over whose *team* I'm gonna be on! They keep saying, "Oh, he's gonna be our *pinch-hitter!*" Like, I couldn't hit a ball if my *life* depended on it! As soon as I step out there, it's OVER! The mask is off and I'm gonna be an IMPOSTER to them. Oh, sure. Sure, it's just a game, but from here on out, I'll be excluded from all the important lunch dates. Shunned at the water cooler. Annette. You know I think you're terrific. In *every* department. You know that. But don't be *too* terrific today. Don't make me look bad. You get what I'm saying? Could you just—for me—go out there today and really *suck?*

INSULATED

I said NO! Look, I *don't* want to *see* her again, okay? (*Beat.*) She's fine, she's beautiful, she's funny ... I just don't wanna *see* her. (*Beat.*) Look, Terry. I know she's your friend and I know you set this whole thing up, but what good will getting involved do anyway, Huh? What the hell will it solve? It's not gonna bring my wife back. It's not gonna ... put her back here, in front of me. (*Beat.*) You know, we used to talk about this ... actually, Helen would talk. I would listen. And try to change the subject. She always thought something was gonna happen to me and she'd be left here. (*Beat.*) Well, it's mighty funny how things turn out, isn't it? 'Cause there I am, filling out orders one day and a call comes through and ... there it is. She's dead. Just like that. Car accident, this voice on the other end says. And that's *it*. (*Beat.*) Did you know that every time I look at the phone, I think of that? Every time I take an order, it comes back to me just as clearly as if it was last week. Every time that phone rings, I think, who is it now? Who are they gonna take away from me now? But you see? There's nobody else that they can take away from me. That's been my goal ever since then. To insulate myself, to ... (*Pause.*) I don't want to have to take one of those calls again, Terry. That's why I will never get involved with anybody, ever again. I just can't do it. I couldn't stand it one more time. Maybe that's really sad, or selfish, to you ... but that is how I've got to live. So tell your friend I had a really nice time the other night. But I can't see her again.

28

KENTUCKY BOURBON

Look, Clem. You've got to stop yodeling all the time. It wasn't so bad, you know, at first, but now ... the neighbors are starting to call at six in the morning, or whenever it is you start, and they're pissed as hell and I don't *blame* them! Maybe it's all right back in Kentucky, but this is New York City, Clem. There are a lot of things that you can't do in an apartment building that I guess you're used to and you just, you've got to understand! Like the raccoon hunting. Clem, people are afraid to leave their rooms. There's a hillbilly maniac running up and down the halls with a shotgun! Last week, you shot somebody's Chihuahua! And even *that* wouldn't have been so bad if you hadn't brought the damn thing back home to *skin* it! How many times do I have to tell you, there are NO RACCOONS in New York City! Now ... I don't *mind* you staying here. You're my fourth cousin and, after all, blood is ... a bond— LISTEN TO ME! If you turn that thing on I swear to God I will KICK THE SPEAKERS IN! I know you gotta make a living, we all do. But these SQUARE DANCING LESSONS have GOT TO STOP! If I have to listen to the Red Clay Ramblers one more time, I'll haul that shotgun out and I'll BLOW YOUR FUCKING HEAD OFF! (*Beat.*) Oh—! I'm sorry! I'm—Oh, God! I didn't mean to get—excited. It's—it's this city, it—it gets to you, it—Hey, look. Let's—let's break out the moonshine and patch things up. Okay?

LAST STRAW

Do you think you could kill somebody? *I* do. Oh, hey, look, I'm sorry! I didn't mean to *scare* you or anything! Like, I *know* that's about the *last* thing you wanna hear on a first date is that the guy sittin' across from you is an axe-murderer or something! Ha. No—no, it's just, sometimes I ... I get kinda mad. You know. And a lotta times I don't have whatcha call an *outlet*. A way to let it out. Like today. I tried to leave work early, 'cause I knew I was gonna be meeting you. S'a blind date, I wanna make a good impression. But I couldn't leave early, I hadda stay 'til five. Okay. Fine. So when I get out, I hurry over to the dry cleaners to get my nice sportcoat—oh, thanks, but this isn't it. No, the *real* one disappeared. See, I give 'em my claim ticket and the dry cleaning guy, he hands me a fuchsia evening gown with beads all over it. And I say, "Buddy, I *think* you made a mistake." 'Cause. You know. (*HE gestures, "Would I wear a dress?"*) But he says it's been misplaced and he won't be able to track it down 'til tomorrow. Okay. Fine. I accept this. I deal with it. I *try to be flexible.* So I run back out to my car—oh, thanks, but that's not *my* car. No, that's my brother Harry's. Yeah, see, when I was inside the dry cleaner's, *my* car got stolen! So I fill out a police report, I run alla way home, I get there and by now it's time to meet you. So I throw on these clothes, slap on some aftershave—oh, thanks, but this isn't what I *usually* wear. No, I knocked mine over into the toilet when I was hurrying to get ready. This is my next-door-neighbor's. Hal's. But you see what I'm trying to say? (*Beat.*) What I'm *trying* to say is, it's already hard enough to meet somebody in this city, and when you finally do, everything just sorta seems to conspire against you—I mean, I feel like one a them—what d'ya call those, salmons?—swimming upstream, fighting and fighting to get to where I'm going and I just—(*Pause.*) Look. I'm sorry I punched-out the waiter. But when he said they were out of taco salad? That was the last straw. It's not a reflection on you. It's just been a bad day.

LEAP OF FAITH

What keeps *me* going? I dunno. Some mornings I just lie in bed and wonder what the hell is going to happen to us. This place seems to be falling to pieces all around us, no matter what we do. All this with the bankruptcy and—well, you know. It all used to be so *easy* and things just seem so weighted down now. Like there's no light at the end of the tunnel all of a sudden. I know things must feel the same way for you, I know they *must*. We think the same. We built this business together on the same ideas. We grew up together, we went to high school together, we went out on our first dates together. Double-dates. Yeah. You remember? The *Drive-In!* (*HE laughs.*) God, that was so long ago. We were so naive ... (*Beat.*) You asked me how I do it. How I get up in the morning and come down here. Call it ... a leap of faith, I guess. It's hard to explain. (*Beat.*) Sometimes I lie there and I think about how hopeless things seem to be. And then I look over at Sharon and I see her sleeping next to me and I remember how good she is and how much I love her ... and *that* just seems to be reason enough for me. That makes me get up and come in here and try one more time. I guess we have to take it one day at a time, Ross. I guess that's the best advice I can give.

METAMORPHOSIS

Don't walk away from me! You can't keep walking away! Yes you do, you keep walking away from *everybody*. From me. From Annie. From Mom ... every time Mom tries to talk to you, you just shut her off! I've watched you—I am *not*! I am not a smartass; you want to know what I am? I'm terrified! I'm scared to death! Everything I know is changing all around me and it's like I don't know you anymore. (*Beat.*) When it first started, we hardly even noticed. You were just coming home late from work. Snapping at all of us. And then, you were coming home later and later ... the snapping turned into shouting. Throwing things. Hitting Mom—I SAW IT! (*Beat.*) You kept telling us, "business is off." Okay, so business is off. We don't care about that! We don't care! We care about *you*. Dad ... we want you back. No, Dad—Dad! You've got a problem. You do, yes, you do. And you've got to admit it. If you'll just *admit* it, we'll help you. We'll stand by you, I swear we will. (*Beat.*) Dad, we *love* you. Please ... Let us love you.

MODERN ROMANCE

My friend Mike told me that the supermarket was a really great place to meet girls. And I said, what the hell are you talking about, but he said, no, really. He said that's where he met Katie and, well, they're *married* now, so I didn't have any reason to doubt him. Plus, I don't exactly have many *prospects* these days, so I drove over to Kroger's just for the hell—excuse me, heck of it, just to see if he was for real. I started in Aisle 3: Canned goods. Got myself a cart and started loading up on peas and cream style corn and peach halves and before you know it, I got a whole cartful of food—plus, there's this beautiful girl, all alone, checking the prices on the black-eyed peas. So I go over there and I start looking too, and we start up this little conversation, and I ask her if she has any *coupons*. Yeah, I thought that might go over well, and she says yeah, you want some? And before I know it, we're *sharing coupons*! And we move on from aisle to aisle and things are really going well! We find out we really have a lot in common and she knows some people I know from college, all kindsa cool stuff like that. And then ... we get to the register. And I realize, oh my God! I didn't bring any *money*! I didn't, you know, plan to *buy* anything, I was just plannin' on meeting a girl! But I don't wanna tell her that, 'cause I don't want her to think I'm, like, some deadbeat or something. So I pretend I have to go back for some styrofoam cups and I leave her up front to check out on her own. Then I ditch that cart full of stuff and get out of there as fast as these legs will carry me! I told her I'd meet her there again in a week. And that's *today*. Now, maybe you think I'm being a little ... *impulsive*, but I don't think so. That's why I came here to see you today. To talk to you. Reverend, I want you to come down there with me and, if she shows up, I want you to marry us right there in the Frozen Foods. 'Cause, see, if you and I walk in there and she's *waiting* for me ... well, then, we're *destined* for each other. Right?

MONEY

I've always loved money. You know? I mean, really *loved* it. Because, as you probably know, money can do a lot of things. It can make a bad day seem good; it can surround you with anything you've ever wanted to own; it can make you the "best friend" of almost any elected official ... in short, you can put yourself into just about *any* position you want to be in. But there are a lot of things that money *can't* do. It can't buy you a lasting relationship with anybody ... and it certainly can't bring you love. When you have a lot of money, you think you've got everything. And then when something like *this* happens ... well, you kinda realize just how superficial your life has been. Ever since I met you—I don't know, this is hard to explain, really—but *money* has meant less and less to me. I guess I should be glad, huh? I mean, some people wait their whole lives to learn something like this and look how young I am! What brought all this on? I don't really know. It's just—when you came up with the whole idea for the dinner party and said you wanted me to invite my six closest friends—remember? I couldn't *think* of six people who were truly close to me. Half a dozen people! For all the money I've got, I don't have half a dozen friends who would really care that I'm engaged. (*Beat.*) So, the party may be a little small this time out ... but, as time goes on, I will make it bigger and bigger until my life is full once again.

MY OWN PLACE

Every time I come back ... this town seems a little smaller. It just keeps shrinking. I used to come home twice a year; my summer vacation and at Christmas. Then I just started coming home at Christmas. And now ... well, I don't get here very often anymore, do I? I know, I know. But once you get outside of a place like this and build your own life, it gets harder and harder to come back. To find *reasons* to come back. I'm not judging you, Griff. I'm not judging *anybody*. You want to stay here, that's fine by me. In a weird way, I actually *respect* you for it. I mean, lookit you—you got a house, a wife and kids, the whole thing. What've I got? A good job. Keeps me travelling. But that's about it. (*Beat.*) I've always envied you a little. You probably envy me too, doncha? You think I'm off, having some kinda adventures or something. Well, I hate to disappoint you, Griff. But I'm not having all that many adventures. I'm just plugging along. Just like everybody else. Just trying to ... to get by. (*Beat.*) Truth is, I always told myself we hadn't changed. That you and I, we hadn't changed. That's been my reason to come back here, ever since Mom and Dad passed on, that was the thing that kept bringing me back here. But I've been lying to myself, Griff. There's no spite in what I'm telling you, you understand? I'm just saying ... we're different now. As different as two people can be. And now that I know that ... Well, I don't think you're gonna be seeing me that much anymore. Sorry. But I gotta find my *own* place. And it's not here.

MY SUIT

What wassat you said to me? Did I *hear* you correctly? No, I want
you to repeat what you just *said.* You said you didn't like my *suit.*
Isn't that what you said? I thought that's what you said. That you
didn't *like* it. Yeah? Well, WHO THE HELL ASKED YOU? Huh?
You think I like that piece a shit *you* got on? It looks like
somethin' my Grandpa was buried in. Uh-huh. Well. You wanna
step outside? I said, you wanna step outside? *Why?* Cause I'm
gonna *show* you. You don't like my suit, I'm gonna *show* you. I
take my clothing *very seriously,* asshole! Uh-huh. I *do!* This is
something I take very seriously. Listen to me: the *last* guy who
didn't like this suit ... I took a twenty-foot length of rope—you
listenin' to me? Good—and I tied it to the bumper of my car. Then I
tied the *other* end to his feet. Then I drove two and a half miles
down a gravel road. And then I let him soak in a bathtub fulla
rubbing alcohol. Over*night.* (*Beat.*) Now. I'm gonna ask you one
more time. I'm gonna ask you again. And *this* time, I want you to
think it over very carefully before you answer ... (*Beat.*) How do
you like my *suit?*

NOTHING TO PROVE

Hey, hey! Whoa, easy, Billy. C'mon ... *No!* (*Beat.*) Look, I don't
wanna play anymore one-on-one. Because. I'm *tired!* I worked all
day and—what? Oh, come *on!* You think I worked that into the
conversation on *purpose?* Jesus, Billy. I mean, what *is* it with you?
Huh? Every day, I come home and we gotta shoot baskets, or we
gotta run three or four miles, or we gotta play tennis—you feel like
you gotta kick my ass in some kinda sport every day and all I wanna
do is crawl inside and plop on my couch. Is that all right with you?
(*Beat.*) Look, Billy. You don't have to beat me every day just to
make a statement. Or whatever it is you're trying to do. You lost
your job. Okay. I don't think less of you because of that. Neither
does Mary. I mean, what, you think we look *down* on you or
something 'cause you got laid *off?* You're my big brother.
Remember? So what, you're outta work? I said you could stay with
us, so you stay. As long as it takes. Bill. You gotta hear me.
'Cause I'll keep saying it until I'm blue in the face: *You have
nothing to prove.* You're my buddy, okay? And I'm here to help
you, no matter what it takes. Now stop being a butthead and let's
go inside and veg a little, okay? (*Beat.*) Okay! Now *that's* the Billy *I*
know.

OBSESSION

So, what, then? You went up there? And what? You talked to her? And what'd she say? She said the same thing, didn't she? I'll bet you she said the same damn thi—Rachel! You are being just *psychotic* about this whole thing! I *never* shoulda told you about Kim. I never should have. Because! You've been following her around like a carrier pigeon! What did I tell you? I told you, Kim and I broke up six years ago! I told you, I have NO DESIRE TO SEE HER AGAIN! And yet you don't believe that. You can't *accept* it! You're *obsessed*! You keep driving out to her house to "check up" on her. Yeah, well, you're lucky she doesn't have you *arrested*. She *could*, you know. She could dial 911 and—NO! I am NOT taking her side! I'm just saying—(*Beat.*) Look. What do you want me to do? To prove to you, once and for all, that it's OVER? You tell me what you want me to do and I will *do* it! You want me to burn all my old photo albums? RIP UP that picture of me and Kim at the high school prom? Stuff it down the GARBAGE DISPOSAL? Will that put this obsession to rest, finally, for once and for all? Because it's OVER, Rachel. I can tell you again and again until I'm blue in the face but you have GOT to believe me! KIM IS NOT A PART OF MY THOUGHTS ANYMORE—IT'S OVER! (*Beat.*) Okay, then. This is settled. Right? We'll never have to talk about this again. Okay? Okay? Good. (*Long pause.*) But since you brought it up ... how'd she *look*?

OLD-FASHIONED GUY

These modern girls don't seem to go for a guy like me. See, I consider myself an old-fashioned guy. You know. I like *beer*. I like *sports* ... I like this maroon sweatshirt with a *hole* in it. If you asked me, what's the last book I read, I'd say ... WHAT BOOK? (*Laughs*.) But seriously, girls these days seem to be turned off by guys like me. They seem to go for the guys who wear glasses and go to health clubs and *read* a lot. Yeah, and drink bottled water. The ones you see on the commuter train, goin' to Wall Street every morning. Yeah. So, I got this idea, see. I went down to Woolworth's and I bought me a cheap pair of reading glasses. And I slicked back my hair and I shaved and I put on a shirt and a tie. Then I noticed that a lotta these guys, these types of guys I'm talking about, they're always reading the Business Section of the *Times*. So I get me the *Times* and I throw out everything but the Business Section. And I start saying "good morning" to some a these cute girls. And *they* start saying it *back*! And guess what? Bingo! After only a week, I got *three dates*! Only ... when we get together, these dates and me? I don't know what to *talk* about! And they don't any of 'em seem to appreciate Pizza Hut or Female Mud Wrestling either. Female Mud Wrestling! Thirty-five dollars *a ticket*, down the tubes! So I said to myself, shit. Why go to *all* that trouble just to be frustrated? So I threw out the glasses, burned the dress shirt, flushed the tie down the toilet, and I put my maroon sweatshirt back on! (*Beat*.) I *still* haven't met anybody. But when I *do* ... I'll know who I *am* now. And I'll at least know she likes me causa that and not causa what paper I read. So gimme the *Post* and let's see the sports section, Andy. Okay?

OLD WIVES' TALE

I think it's all a misconception. I do. I think you have been totally misled by your peers, your parents, the Entertainment Industry. This whole Sex Thing! Do you really believe that men crave sex *all the time*? No. That's a myth. It's like, some Old Wives' Tale. A Fable. I mean, if Freud only knew what he did to modern society by sitting around *theorizing* ... I mean, here we are. We've been out—what? Three times now? And it's been great! But you don't have to feel threatened. Because I have *never* wanted to sleep with you. *(Beat.)* Well, I take that back. Maybe once. Right at first—But I'm not a wolf or anything! I haven't sat around, fantasizing about seeing you in sexy lingerie for hours on end like the women in those Victoria's Secret catalogues ... *(Beat.)* Okay, well, maybe a little. But not obsessively or anything. I think women have been led to believe that men are, are animals. That we look at you purely as objects— which we don't—when the truth of the matter is, we—*I*, anyway— look at you as an equal! That's right, an equal! When we're sitting here talking, what? You think I'm not listening, you think I'm busy picturing you naked, writhing in my arms or something? Hah! *(Beat.)* Well, okay, the image *has* crossed my mind a few times ... *(Beat.)* Look, Annie. You're a beautiful woman. That's the bottom line. You are strikingly stunning. But I'm fully aware that you wish to be treated as a person, not an object. Okay. Fine. Great. We've said it. It's been defined. The definitions are all out on the table. I am perfectly prepared to treat you like you want to be treated, that's not a problem. I'm just telling you, if that's the case ... I'm going to have to do *one thing*: I'm going to have to wear a blindfold. *(Takes a blindfold out of his pocket, puts it on.)* But please. Don't think of me any differently.

OUT HERE

I'd rather be in *jail*, man. I'd rather be in there than out *here*. This ain't no shit I'm tellin' you. I was in the State Pen for seventeen months and I swear to God, I'd rather be back there any day of the week. Why the fuck you think? Huh? Fuckin' *parole* officer ... what does that son of a bitch know? He's gonna get me a job. That's what he kept tellin' me. I finally say, okay. So *get* me a job. You wanna *get* me a job, you *get* me a damn job, man. Next thing I know, I'm flippin' hamburgers in that fuckin' fast food place. Fella who calls hisself a "manager" keeps breathing down my neck: "if you got time to lean, you got time to clean." I said, fuck *you* you stupid son of a bitch! Like, I'm gonna take shit off that slimeball for three dollars an hour? No way, man. No fuckin' *way*! I'd rather be back in jail than tied down to *that* kinda shit. I swear ta God! (*Beat.*) Look. I wasn't gonna *kill* the guy. I just wanted to teach him a fuckin' lesson! I didn't want him breathin' down my *neck*! You hear what I'm sayin'? 'Sides, I didn't *shoot* the gun! I just pulled it on him! (*Beat.*) Lissen. If I wanted him to be dead, he'd be dead now. I only wanted ... (*Beat.*) Look. You wanna know why I did it? I'll *tell* you why I did it: I *did* it 'cause I wanna go back. I wanna go back. I was *used* to it in there ... But, man, I can't take it out *here*.

OVER MY DEAD BODY

HOW? (*Beat.*) How? *How*? HOW? *HOW* did we manage to accumulate all this *crap*? I have been packing since nine o'clock last night and I had—forgive me—fallen under the ridiculous assumption that we were *almost through*! And now—this! Where were you *hiding* all these things? On the roof? In the guest room? Look at that! That vacuum cleaner hasn't worked since *Nixon* was in office! And that sleeping bag ... you haven't zipped yourself up in it since you were twelve years old! And that! What *is* that, a bean bag chair? My God! Where does all this stuff *come* from? Does it crawl behind the paneling and hide under the foundation of our home? Or do you tuck it away on purpose, just to spite me? You know how I hate *accumulating* things! You *know* I hate it! God, I can't believe you've *saved* all this crap! I feel like I'm trapped on the set of *Sanford & Son*. We should be opening a junk shop, not moving to San Fran—No! No *way*! Touch those and you die. You are *not* taking those Bobby Sherman records. Sharon! We have enough clutter already! Now, I mean it! I am *not* playing games here! We are not taking *any* of this stuff—*any* of it!—and that's final! (*Beat.*) What? Leave—what? Leave my—what? My *bowling trophies*? Over my DEAD BODY!

PARTY PSYCHOLOGY

WHAT? (*Beat.*) I'M SORRY, I CAN'T HEAR YOU OVER THE MUSIC! COULD YOU YELL A LITTLE LOUDER? I SAID— (*Listens.*) YEAH, THAT'S BETTER! WHAT'S YOUR NAME AGAIN? YOUR NAME. NAME! (*Beat.*) QUINT? QUI—WHAT? OH—OH, *CLINT*! HI, CLINT. I'M GEORGE. *GEORGE*! G-E-O—OH, NEVER MIND! (*Reacts to a change in the "noise level."*) Ooh, now that's better. Now I can hear my ears ringing. Nice to meet you, Clint. Yeah, I usually don't go to parties much. Oh, my wife's here, she's off *mingling* ... someplace. (*Looks around.*) There she is! She's a mingler, all right. Sounds like a kind of *fish,* eh? (*Laughs.*) Yeah, well, the way I see it, there are three types of Party People: Floaters, Latchers, and Sinkers. My wife, now, *she's* a Floater. Floats all over the place, bouncing from person to person, talking, chatting. Real friendly and outgoing—there she is again. (*Waves.*) Hi, honey! (*Back to "Clint."*) Then you got your Latchers, who are pretty uncomfortable about being at parties. They don't know how to mix well, so they attach themselves—latch on—to a Floater and hang on for dear life, letting the Floater carry 'em around all night. They panic when their Floater has to go to the bathroom or something 'cause then they're left stranded all by themselves and they don't know how to make conversation. And that's when they become Sinkers. See, I *used* to be a Latcher. Now I'm a Sinker. A Sinker sinks like a rock to the bottom of the aquarium and just sits there with the rest of the rocks. You and me, eh? Oh, no, no. That's not an *insult*, Clint, that's a *compliment*! Yeah, I think so. I'd rather be a Sinker than a Floater. Wouldn't you? Damn right! (*Long pause as HE just stands there, unsure of what to say.*) Helluva party, eh? Yeah ... (*Reacts to the "noise" again.*) UH-OH! THEY TURNED THAT *MUSIC* UP AGAIN! (*Beat.*) I SAID, THEY TURNED THAT MUSIC UP AGAIN! (*Beat.*) I SAID—NEVER MIND. (*Stands there a moment, uncomfortable.*) HELLUVA PARTY!

43

PERFECT EXAMPLE

I don't know quite what to say here. (*Beat.*) No, I am. I *am* impressed. I'm *very* impressed. Yes. Oh, what you've done has made a *great* ... impression on me. But I think what you have to understand is—. Look. I say those kinds of things a *lot*. All the time. It's what you'd call second nature with me. I don't think about it, they just come out. I'm always walking around, offering people a dollar to do *this*, or five bucks to do *that*, you know. It's kind of a—what? No, not a *dare*, exactly, more of a *joke*. (*Beat.*) Well, see, like I've been saying since we met. You sometimes take me a little too *seriously*. And this is a perfect example. When I said I'd give you twenty bucks to take all your clothes off in the middle of the Museum, I was just kidding! I didn't mean for you to actually *do* it—! Oh no, no! I am *not* ashamed of your body! Of course not. You're ... well, you are *much* better looking than anything in the Hall of 20th Century Nudes. But I just think that now is a good time to reach an understanding on this issue—before it *becomes* an issue. 'Cause if, in the heat of anger, let's say I offer you fifty bucks to *shoot* somebody or something ... (*Beat.*) Well, you see what I mean? I *love* you, and I don't want you to end up behind bars just because you took me too seriously!

PETS

I will never take care of anybody's pets again as long as I live! Jerry Rosenfeld, guy who worked in my office? Says to me, "George, will you look after my cat while I'm away?" And so I say, "Sure." Next day, he says, "Oh, hey, I forgot to mention. I have a *dog* too." Well, okay. Sure. I *said* I'd do it, I'm not gonna back out. But then, each day, he "remembers" another pet that he "forgot" to mention the day before: a goldfish, a *bird*, a BOA CONSTRICTOR! But I'm still trying to be a n*ice guy* about the whole thing, so even though I'm starting to get a little shaky, I say okay. Well, to make a long story short, Jerry Rosenfeld goes to Bermuda for five days. One of those singles places? While he's gone, he meets the Love of His Live. Fine. But I'm left with what I can only describe as an indoor zoo! First day I'm there, I try to take the dog out for a walk; the cat gets out. I go downstairs and get the cat and I bring it back up and lock it in the bathroom while I feed the fish. I look for the bird, but the cat knocked over the cage trying to eat the bird. So I hang the birdcage up and go to let the cat out of the bathroom. But the snake, which lived in the tub, has devoured the cat. Meanwhile, the dog has peed all over the hardwood floor because it got its hopes up that it was gonna go for a walk. So I mop up the dog pee but while I'm doing that I accidentally knock over the birdcage with the mop handle. The bird has a stroke and dies—but that's not the WORST of it! 'Cause by now, the SNAKE is slithering into the room and looking at me and flicking its tongue. So I lock the door and leave the dog and the snake to battle it out. I'm sure the snake finished off the dog. Four days later, Jerry Rosenfeld comes home, sees the devastation, has a heart attack, and dies. (*Beat.*) So, no. I will not take care of your hamster, Scott. Nothing good can come of it.

PRIMITIVE MAN

How did Man survive before frozen dinners came along? Did you ever think about that? Before Salisbury Steak, Fried Chicken Nuggets, Turkey & Dressing. Mmmm. Well, I'll tell you: he cooked from scratch. Oh, yes! Surprising as it sounds. He killed animals and roasted their flesh. Ripped green leaves up out of the earth and munched them into photosynthetic mulch! And then he swallowed *(HE does so.)*, digested, and eliminated the excess. And he went on with his life. *(Beat.)* Well, I wish I were Primitive Man right about now. Because all we have EATEN for the last SEVEN MONTHS are TV DINNERS! I CANNOT STAND IT ANYMORE! I feel like Swanson, Morton, and Mrs. Paul are MEMBERS OF THIS FAMILY! If I have to put one more bite of plum cobbler on my tongue—*(HE gags.)* Darlene. I haven't had a bowel movement in two weeks! I have to eat something fresh, something *green*, or I am certain that I am going to die! I know, I know, "it's the age of convenience." But it isn't the age I want to live in. So could we please eat a salad? Or a banana or a grapefruit, or—what? You—what? You bought ... *watermelon*? Oh, God, Darlene! Primitive Man would be so *proud* of you!

ROMANTIC

Van Gogh cut off his ear. They say. That's what they *say*. For the love of a beautiful woman, he cut his ear off. But if I did something like that, you'd puke. Wouldn't you? Times have changed, Rachel. I *want* to be romantic, but whenever I try, it seems like I'm in the wrong era or something. (*Beat.*) I send four dozen roses to your office ... and they arrive right in the middle of your corporate business meeting, destroying all your credibility as a tough tradesperson. (*Makes a "buzzer" sound.*) Strike one. (*Beat.*) A week later, I stand outside your apartment building to serenade you ... and your upstairs neighbor throws a metal trash can off his balcony at me to shut me up! Three weeks I'm in the hospital with a cracked-open head. I get laid off my job 'cause they learn how to deal without me those three weeks so *now* I don't have an income and I'm so busy watching every penny that I can't afford to take you out anymore! (*"Buzzer" sound again.*) Strike Two. (*Beat.*) I *finally* scrape together enough money to take you out to a nice dinner. And there we were, an hour ago, sitting in a Japanese restaurant. I kneel down to propose to you ... and a two-inch nail goes sticking through the floorboard into my kneecap! (*Beat.*) I *want* to be a romantic guy, Rachel, I really, really do. But the twentieth century just doesn't seem to be the place for that! (*Beat.*) Listen ... I know this hospital room is pretty antiseptic. It's not very special ... but will you marry me? (*Beat.*) You *will*? Oh, Rachel! I'm so happy! (*An idea:*) What do you say we have the ceremony *here*? In the waiting room? I know, I know, it may not be very *romantic* ... but then again, who needs romantic? I'd like to do something *right* for a change!

SELF-RESPECT

I don't understand it. My daddy wouldn't understand it either.
They're payin' us *not* to grow crops. (*Beat.*) Which, in a way, is
fine. I mean, *I* need the money. God knows we *all* need the money.
But we also need to *work*. I need to work. A man's *got* to work!
(*Beat.*) You can't sit around all day, day after day, doin' nothin'!
You just can't! It eats away at your self-respect. Like cancer. I seen
it happen. You remember ol' Nob Young? Worked at the airplane
plant. That man was the most hard-workin' individual I believe I've
ever seen in my life! Big ol' strong fella, with bright blue eyes.
Well ... they let him go, coupla years ago. Cutbacks. Told him he
was too old. Hell, he's only fifty-eight. Strong as any eighteen-year-
old you could find. Worked all his life, since he's fourteen. Last
time I seen him ... seems like he'd aged twenty years. His eyes ...
his eyes, that was always so lit up ... they looked dead. I bet you he
don't live five more years. A man like that can't sit around, idle all
the time. A man has *got* to work! That's how he identifies himself!
(*Thinks a moment.*) But a man's gotta *eat,* too ... So. What'm I
supposed to tell these people? After all, it's the Government we're
talkin' about. They wanna give me all this money *not* to farm the
acreage. And they're gonna *want* an answer.

SENSE OF FAMILY

You miss your family. You can sit here and *tell* me that you don't miss 'em, but I *know* you miss your family. *(Beat.)* I told you about how *I* left home. I said to hell with all of 'em and I just left. Moved out here, started over ... My first job was cold-calling. For some fly-by-night insurance company. Yeah. Picking up a receiver four hundred times a day, going down a list of numbers. Calling. Day after day, hundreds and hundreds of telephone numbers on this big computer printout they stole from someplace, it all turned into one big grey blur. I think I made minimum wage or something. Anyway, after about two weeks of this my brain had turned into oatmeal. I was this zombie: "Hello, my name is Tim, I'm calling from Colonial Life and Casualty ..." I got to where I was saying that in my *sleep!* Well, one day I'm dialing numbers and I'm giving my schpiel. I hadn't sold a thing in two, three days and I know they were about to can me. So I dial the phone and some woman answers and I say, "Good afternoon, my name is Tim, I'm calling from Colonial Life and Casu—" And on the other end, I hear my *mother* say "Tim? Is that *you?*" And my heart stopped. My eyes raced down the printout, down this endless river of dot-matrix numbers, to see what the hell number I had dialed. And there it was, right in front of me ... my mom's first initial, last name and phone number. Buried right there with all those thousands of others. I tried to talk, but I couldn't. I just started crying. I don't know why, but I just started crying. Hung up. I couldn't *talk,* I didn't know what to *say. (Beat.)* I never talked to her again and she ... well, she died about six months later. *(Beat.)* I thought I was *so tough.* I told myself over and over again, I didn't miss 'em. But I did. And I still do. So don't tell me you don't miss your family. I know it's a lie.

SEVEN LITTLE WORDS

Do you know what I've done? I have just *castrated* myself! Well, *figuratively*! I just went in there and opened my *big mouth* in front of the whole office staff! And with seven little words—"I don't care about the Super Bowl"—I castrated myself. (*Beat.*) Or is that *six* words ...? Is Super Bowl *one* word, or *two*? (*Beat.*) I am *not* being "silly"! I am totally serious! You don't understand, Mary. This is one of those Male Things. Like—like joining the Boy Scouts and traipsing through the woods, getting chewed up by insects! Or—or being dragged to a Bachelor Party where a tired old stripper takes her clothes off and everybody screams like animals. Huh? Oh, Mike's wedding. Yeah. But what I'm trying to say is, a guy shouldn't *ever* admit that he doesn't *care* about the World Series or the Super Bowl. I don't know what got into me! We were just talking and—and it just slipped out! See, there's some kind of an unspoken code or something with the guys in this office and there are certain boundaries you don't cross if you know what's good for you and ... and I just crossed them. Now I'll never be taken seriously again. I'll never be treated fairly. I'll always be picked on. I can see it now ... sooner or later, they'll be standing around the water cooler, imitating me with a *lisp* tacked onto my voice. I'll probably lose the key to the executive washroom. I'll probably get laid off! I'll probably—what? He *what*? The boss doesn't like *what*? He doesn't like *sports*? My God ... (*Beat.*) What kind of a man is *he*?

SILENCE

I know this probably looks boring to you. But I like it. Greg and
some of my brother's friends say I'm "unmotivated" and that I'm
gonna be earning minimum wage for the rest of my life. Now that's
not true, but even if it was, so *what*? I *like* it here. That's
something that nobody seems to grasp, or *wants* to grasp. I like this
counter. I like those books. I like the card *catalogue*! (*Realizing
HE's gotten too loud, HE gets quieter:*) I even like the *silence*.
Listen. (*Pause.*) You can *hear the silence.* I think I like that best of
all. (*Beat.*) It wasn't like this in the NYPD. You didn't know about
that, did you? Yeah, well, I guess that's my one well-guarded secret.
I didn't know what else to do, I was right outta high school and,
well, *you've* met my dad. He's *so* Blue Collar. He encouraged me to
do it. (*Beat.*) My first week on the street, I killed somebody. It was
just like one a those TV shows. Cop shows. You know. Guy
robbing a convenience store ... we get the call ... he starts shooting.
I had to stop him. Period. That's what I *had to do*. So I stopped
him. (*Beat.*) I can still hear those shots. They still ring in my head.
That was the most awful sound I've ever heard in my life. And the
blood ... (*HE shudders.*) So. For now, I *want* to be a librarian. You
understand? At least *this* way when I go home at night ... I know
I'm gonna be going home *alive*.

SURPRISES

I'm not gonna tell you again! This is absolutely the last time I'm going to say it! I'm not dressing up like a *pumpkin*. (*Beat*.) Look. I know it's Halloween and I know things are supposed to be *festive* ... but I am not getting into that costume. I am grateful—believe me, I am incredibly grateful—that you've spent the last two weeks *making* it, but I wish to God you'd *told* me first. It comes as—as kind of a shock. To see that. To be told you're supposed to—to *wear* that. Maureen. Look. I'm a fat guy. Okay. Large. I'm a large guy. And when you try to dress a large guy up to look like a *pumpkin*—HE HAS A TENDENCY TO FEEL KIND OF LIKE A FUCKING IDIOT! OKAY? (*Beat*.) You've gotta quit doing this. *Surprising* me. I told you way back when we first met, I DON'T LIKE SURPRISES. I thought you'd have learned your lesson last summer. The surprise birthday? Yeah, when I had that heart attack? I thought I was being assaulted! How did I know those strange men were bringing me here to be *surprised*! And then there was that time when you painted the bathroom *black* ... I woke up one morning and thought I'd gone *blind*! (*Beat*.) I appreciate the thought that goes into these ... these *ideas*. But, please. From now on? Just *tell* me ahead of time. Okay? I think we'll *both* live a lot longer that way.

TOILET HUMOR

You *used* to think it was funny. You used to think farting sounds were *hilarious*. (*HE makes one.*) Now all you do is make that disgusted face, like somebody tried to put a cockroach on your tongue or something. Oh, c'mon! I am *not that bad*! I'm not as bad as *most* of the people I know. Like Ed and Bennie? (*Beat.*) They are *not* assholes! They're my friends! (*Beat.*) Ooooh. Oh, I see. I see where this is heading. I have to *choose*, eh? This is one of those things. Where it all comes down to you or them, huh? Is that it? Well, I'll tell you something: I can't! I can't *choose*. You're all a part of me. I mean, I love going to museums and plays with you and reading Dostoevski and all that ... but I also love a good, crude dose of TOILET HUMOR every once in a while. (*HE burps.*) Okay. I get the point. You are NOT going to laugh, are you? Uh-huh. Well, then. Maybe you've got it all backwards, Charlene. Ever think of that? Well, maybe it's not *me* that has to choose here. Maybe it's *you*. You wanted me to choose between culture and toilet humor, between you or them. Maybe *you're* the one who has to make a choice: Me or nothing. Fart sounds ... or silence. Now you *think* before you make a decision, because you should realize that, in the great scheme of things ... a few fart sounds aren't all that bad. (*HE does one, raises eyebrows to see the result.*)

TRAPPED

Yeah, it was pretty much a shock to me, too. How did I handle it? Let's put it this way: you don't want to do what I did. Well, you asked for my advice, I'm just telling you! Hell, I panicked! Like I'm sure you're doing right now. I panicked and I couldn't see *anything*. It was like my life was over, and I didn't want to talk about it or try to find solutions. I just wanted to END it. I went to the bank and took out everything I had—fifteen hundred dollars—and I put it in an envelope and I stuck it under Cathy's door. And then I got the hell outta Dodge as fast as my pickup would carry me. I guess I was too scared to be around when—you know. (*Beat.*) But she didn't use the money for an abortion. That was all *my* idea, see. No, she had the baby. And now she's married and lives out in some nice subdivision and has two station wagons and two more kids. I got drunk and went out there one night a coupla years ago, firin' a shotgun in the air and carryin' on out in the street like a damn fool. Screaming, "Aaron is mine! He's my son!" I don't know what I hoped to accomplish. I don't even know why I went *out* there. Just got to feeling sorry for myself, I guess. Feeling like I didn't have any *roots*, or anything—I dunno. (*Beat.*) No, it was a *stupid* thing to do. 'Cause now if I go within five hundred yards of their house, one phone call and—BANG—I'm in jail. Jimmy, man, you gotta *think* about this. I know you don't wanna be *trapped*, I know that. But I'm trying to tell you: running away is gonna trap you even more. You gotta find a way to *settle* this ... or it's gonna eat away at you for the rest of your *life*.

WE DREW STRAWS

You have a cat, don't you, Clark? *Two*, huh? Hmm ... Well, have you ever noticed how they, ah, how they sniff each other's *butts* and stuff? Oh, yeah, it's gross, I know, I know, but they *love* things that stink. *Cats* do. Their own vomit ... litter boxes ... bad breath. My cat Theo loves to smell my breath when I first wake up in the morning. Sick, isn't it? What I'm getting at is ... well, people—*people* don't like these things. The, the way these things *smell*. People, as a rule, try to *distance* themselves from, from each other's butts. And other things, things that—that, you know, smell bad. Like, if I were to come to work with bad breath, I would hope someone would *say* something to me. Something like, "Melvin, for God's sake, brush your friggin' teeth!" Or, *something* like that. You know? I would *want* them to. I mean, I wouldn't wanna walk around with bad breath all morning! I mean ... (*Beat.*) Look, Clark. We, ah, we all drew straws, see? We all drew straws and, and I lost. And I'm supposed to tell you ... Remember the other day when you found that deodorant in your desk drawer? Yeah, well, some people in the office put it there. No, no, I can't name names, but, see, they're trying to tell you ... and you just don't seem to *get* it. They've been trying to tell you for *months* now. You've got to *do* something about this, this *thing*. (*Beat.*) Now don't get mad at me, Clark, I don't want you to be *mad*. We drew straws and I lost, and it's just ... well, when a guy sees his cats sniffing each others' butts and thinks of *you* ... well, you kinda have to *do* something about it. Am I right?

WONDERFUL DREAMS

You never met my mother, did you? Well, she was a neat lady. Nothing special to look at. And she certainly wasn't someone who dangled a long list of accomplishments in front of you all the time. She had no resume, she had no stock portfolio ... she was just a—a good, simple, honest soul. Anyway, she, ah, she died last year. Well, you knew that. Yeah. But do you know what she told me right before she passed on? This is weird. She told me she had always wanted to learn how to fly. A *plane*! Isn't that funny? For years, she wanted to be a pilot, but she never told any of us. You have to understand, here's a woman whose husband died not long after I was born, so I practically saw her—we all saw her—as this *spinster* all our lives. This plain little woman, we didn't know she harbored all these wonderful dreams. (*Beat*.) Well, I've got some wonderful dreams too. But I've learned a lesson from Mom. She taught me a big, big lesson: don't let go of your dreams. (*Beat*.) People at work, they think I'm some kinda nut. I told them I wanted to quit and go live on a sailboat for a year and they just—they don't *get* it. I don't think it's nutty, it's what I want to *do*. (*Beat*.) I don't want to be like Mom. I'm not going to let go of my dream.

WORK ETHIC

Dad always told us that if you worked really hard, you'd make it, remember? "Simple as that, boys and girls," he'd say. His good old American work ethic, eh? You remember him telling us how our great-grandfather started selling screws and nails from a pushcart? And how that turned into Grandfather's hardware store and how that turned into Dad's chain of stores? (*Beat.*) Is it just me, or is it really sad that things don't work that way anymore? Not from what *I* can tell, anyway. From what *I* can see, all that matters is that you're charming, smooth, empty, selfish, and a good liar. (*Beat.*) I guess he wanted me to have the "business" since I was the boy, Cathy. Sorry. Couldn't help that. But you must know that I tried to hang onto it. With every means I could think of. But I guess I didn't play dirty enough. These big shots who came in to buy us out knew all the tricks in the book. Had a whole team of fancy two-hundred-dollar-an-hour lawyers in tow. Mr. Anderson, Dad's attorney, is a pretty good lawyer, I guess, but he wasn't prepared for the likes of this. When Dad died and this whole takeover thing started—when the stores went up for sale—Mr. Anderson and I agreed that we wanted to be honest and deal fairly, from the start. To handle things in a way that would make Dad proud. But, in the end, their greed and ambition won out over our good motives. Their power and shrewdness won out over our sense of trust. (*Beat.*) Dad's name'll still be on all those stores, Cathy. At least for awhile. And we're going to get a huge settlement for the whole deal. I don't know why I'm complaining, I guess it all worked-out fine. I just feel like somehow ... something was lost in the whole process. And if Dad's out there, somewhere, watching everything right now ... I'm sure he mourns for the loss of what he once built.

WORLDS APART

Chet? Chet, look. I don't want people to get the wrong idea. Chet!
Hey! You've had a lot to drink, okay? Maybe we'd better—*Chet.*
Look. You told me you were upset, your mother forgot your
birthday ... I *said* I'd come out for a coupla drinks, okay? Fine. I *did*
that. Now I gotta go *home.* I gotta *work* tomorrow! Chet, I'm not
like you. I can't stay out all night and stumble in at half past six,
talking to myself. I can't *do* that. Chet, c'mon. Don't. No. *Chet.*
DON'T HUG ME. (*Beat.*) Chet, look. I don't want anybody to get
the wrong idea, okay? You know what I mean. You keep trying to
hug me and—and, I mean, look where we *are.* Chet. (*Whispered.*)
You brought me to a Gay Bar! "Boots and Stirrup"? Come *on*!
(*Back to regular voice now.*) No. Stop it. Chet. Stay over there.
Stay over there by the cigarette machine and LISTEN. (*Apparently
HE backs into someone.*) Excuse me. (*Back to Chet.*) A second ago,
I said I'm not like you. I was referring to the fact that you're a
Night Owl and I'm not. But Chet ... I'm not like you in a *lotta*
ways and it's time you acknowledged that. Chet, we are worlds
apart, you and I. Sure, sure, we're friends, but I dunno. I'm afraid
you see something *more* there and there's not, okay? There's just—
not. Look, why don't you talk to that guy Steven? He looks like a
nice guy. He's what? *Married*? He looks gay to me. (*Beat.*) Ooooh.
Well, what about that other guy. (*Points.*) Richard. You did? And
what'd he say? Huh. Well, is there *anybody* here you know? Only
me? Great. Okay, all right, look. One more drink. And then I really
gotta go. The only reason I'm doing this is I don't want you to be
sitting in this place all alone. You got that? That's the *only* reason.
Okay. Let's go back to the table. And Chet? Chet. DON'T sit in
my lap again.

YOUNG FOREVER

We agreed, I know, I know, we *agreed* we'd wait for our 20th, wait until we'd ... "made our fortunes." Please, quit reminding me, I know, I know. "Who wants to see all those assholes anyway? We saw enough of 'em in high school," right? That's what we *said. But* ... (*Beat.*) I came across this ... ah, this clipping. Newspaper clipping. Actually, my folks sent it to me. Jeff Stone. You remember him? Yeah, you do. "Putz." We called him "The Putz." Yeah, well ... he got killed. (*Beat.*) I mean, killed. Shot. *Killed.* He went into a Quick Stop for a can of motor oil and just as he went up to the counter to pay for his 10-W-40 ... BANG! He's shot dead by some punk who's robbing the joint. You never know what can happen, Mark. I mean, maybe we're kidding ourselves, y'know? We keep saying that we don't wanna see all these people ... maybe we're just fulla shit. I mean, I *know* we said we wanted to wait until we had something we could go back and "show off" to everybody ... but that's not what it's all about. I mean, I read that clipping about Putz and it hit me: we may never *see* some of these people again. Ever. (*Beat.*) Well, we're not gonna see Jeff Stone again, are we? (Beat.) We shared something with these people. Even the ones we didn't like. We shared a part of our life. And it doesn't matter if we own a million bucks or a hundred bucks when we go back, nobody cares about that. Not really. They just wanna see us again. As much as we wanna see them. I know we keep saying we don't wanna see 'em, but we want to. Don't you? *I* want to. (*Beat.*) So what are we waiting for? Our 10th High School Reunion is *tomorrow* ... Let's just go. Let's see everybody. We're not gonna be young forever.

YOUR CHOICE

Why are you in such a hurry? Busy ... Okay, you're busy—but I only want a coupla minutes! Can I have two minutes? Okay, *one minute*! *Will you just give me one lousy minute*? (*Beat.*) Okay. Now, you have a choice. We *all* have a choice. That's why we're Americans. That is why we live in the greatest democracy in the world. Because we have these choices. What choices are these? Freedom. Freedom to choose. For instance. You could decide ... to walk across the street and shoot one of those people to death. That's your choice. But, the law says that you are to be brought to trial and punished for something like that. What happens then? I'll tell you what happens: Enter me. I ask the witnesses to testify against you. I ask them to make a choice. They can refuse to testify. Fine. In which case you're probably going to go free and you'll probably shoot somebody else. What I hope, however, is that they will make the choice to testify against you. Because along with their ability to choose ... their freedom of choice ... comes responsibility. And our responsibility as free citizens of this democracy is to stand up and tell the truth. No, no, now *you* wait just a second! You saw a woman *murdered*, Mr. Carmichael! You saw it! (*Beat.*) Now, I want to *send* that murderer to prison! And you can help me do that. You want to hide behind a mask which says you are a busy man. Fine. You *do* that. But even busy men have responsibilities ... and even busy men must make choices. So. What's it going to be? It's your choice.

WOMEN

AM I NEXT?

You are dangerous. I see that now. They all *warned* me ... but I didn't listen to any of them. No, don't come any closer! (*Beat.*) When you first came here, they said I'd better watch out for you. And my God, they weren't *lying*! (*Beat.*) I was gone two weeks. And in that short time, you killed Hunter *and* Blake! I honestly didn't think you were *capable* of that. I guess I'm naive, but I never thought they'd let you get away with something like that. And Natasha! You gave her this—this incurable *disease*? (*Beat.*) I live in fear now, Charles. Don't tell me not to WORRY! I was so worried last night I couldn't *sleep*! I FEAR FOR MY LIFE! I mean, if you could get rid of Blake just like that—(*SHE snaps her fingers.*)— what about *me*? WHAT ABOUT ME? Listen, you little putz! Blake was the most original character *on* this damn show! He was one of the few people who made Soaps exciting! Now where's he gonna surface? Some bad sitcom? Some made-for-cable movie? WHO THE HELL DO YOU THINK YOU ARE, CHARLES? You just got out of *college* for chrissakes, and here you are, PLAYING WITH PEOPLE'S LIVES! I don't know how you got this job, but you have a responsibility! As an Executive Producer, you have a responsibility to the viewers, to the stars, to—NO! DO *NOT* COME ANY CLOSER! I'LL SCREAM! (*Beat.*) All I want ... is an explanation. On page 40 of script #2944, the stage directions read: "Monique goes into a coughing fit." (*Beat.*) Now you look me in the eye and you tell me ... AM I NEXT?

BETSY BOOKWORM

Nah, nah ... you go on ahead. I've got a lotta reading to do. *(Beat.)*
Look, if I wanted to go, Adale, I'd *go*. I just ... I don't want to go.
Look. See? I've got three mysteries I've got to get through by
Monday. An Agatha Christie and a—"Why?" What do you mean,
"Why?" Because I LIKE THEM! I LIKE TO READ! *(Beat.)* I'm not
like you, Adale. You're always darting off on a Singles Weekend.
What's this one? "Weekend in the Sand?" Yeah, well ... thanks, but
no thanks. I guess I just prefer being alone sometimes. No, no, not
all the time! God! I just—*(Beat.)* I don't know how to *talk* to
people, Adale. You *do*. I don't know how to look at a guy so that
he'll come over and ask me what's-my-name. You're *great* at all
that! You always *have* been. You're great at cutting loose out there
and making all your own adventures happen. I guess I've always
found *my* adventures here. In books. I've always been like I am.
You've always been like *you* are. *(Beat.)* When I was growing up,
all the other kids called me "Betsy Bookworm." But I *liked* being
Betsy Bookworm! Believe it or not, I still *do*! *(Beat.)* So don't feel
sorry for me. Just go. Have a good time. I'll be here ... when you
get back.

BORIS

We used to have this cat. Big fat red cat named Boris. But he only had three legs. Two and a half, actually. The fourth one and half of the third one got chewed off in fights or something, I can't remember. He was pretty wild. The point is, he couldn't always get around so well. Up and down stairs and everything? He sort of hobbled and crawled wherever he went. But he'd *do* it. He'd get to where we wanted to go. Because he was determined. It might take him fifteen or twenty minutes to get up the stairs to my room, but he'd get there. Fight his way up there and cry until I picked him up and put him in the bed with me. (*Beat.*) You used to be like that. I don't mean crippled. I mean—you know what I mean. Persistent! God, you were persistent. When I first met you? I envied your ability to forge ahead. You never let anyone or anything stop you. I think that's one of the reasons I fell in love with you. (*Beat.*) What happened? It's like you don't even *try* to get up the stairs anymore. I know things have been rough lately, you hate working down there, I know, it's really been awful, but you gotta keep trying. You gotta. Come here. I've got something to show you. Old home movies of Boris in action. I think it might just do you some good to see him conquer those stairs.

COUGH DROPS

You did *what*? You *ate* my COUGH DROPS? Good God, Melvin! This is the last straw! You're, like, a Human Vacuum Cleaner. If it isn't nailed down, whoosh, it goes right into your *gullet*! I can't believe you! Here I am, shopping for groceries THREE TIMES A WEEK now! Letting your pants out ... your underwear—I am *not* a seamstress! Do you have any idea how hard it is TO LET UNDERWEAR OUT? But I do it. I shop and I cook and I serve it up and I hunch over the sewing machine 'till dawn so that you can waddle off to work at Donut World and EAT SOME MORE! And what do I ask for in return? A little compassion? A hug and a kiss now and then? Very little. And here I am, knocked flat on my ass with the worst head cold I have ever had in my life, spitting up bowlfuls of phlegm ... and you tell me you've eaten my LAST BOX OF COUGH DROPS? You have given me no choice. You have to know that you are the one who's driven me to desperate measures. Next time I go shopping ... no more Little Debbies! (*Beat.*) Just remember, Melvin. You brought this on yourself!

DETAILS

I'm not very good with details. Not very good at all. This is my first wedding—well, you *know* it's my first wedding, 'cause I'm the one getting *married*. Of course, these days, that doesn't mean a whole heck of a lot, does it? I mean, look at Liz Taylor. Husband number twenty-three or whatever. Did I tell you I didn't *want* to be in charge of this? I did *not* want to be in charge of this at *all*. I'm so awful at managing things. My checkbook. My *life*. So Ben—my fiance—he said I *should* be in charge of the wedding, 'cause he thought it might teach me a lesson or something. How to be organized. So, Ben and I set the date and he handed it all over to me. I did pretty good, too. I surprised myself. I ordered the invitations and I picked out a cake and I chose a church and I met with the minister and I had the bridesmaids' dresses designed and I ordered the men's tuxedos and I picked out the floral arrangements ... I never dreamed I could actually do all *that*—but I did! I laid out all these plans, set up everything, and Ben was right, you know. An experience like this really does show you that it's best to just jump right in and *do* it. Even if it seems more than you can bite off and chew, you just try. It may be quite a jawbreaker, but you'll *learn* from it. The only problem is ... in making all these plans and organizing this whole thing ... there's one thing I seem to have forgotten about. *Ben.* I don't know where he is, or if he even still plans to *marry* me. We had been spending twenty-four hours a day together, but once I got immersed in this *planning* ... I *lost track* of him. Isn't that awful? (*Beat.*) But like I said, I've learned a *lot*.

DIRTY LOOKS

I'm sick and tired of people giving me dirty looks. (*Beat.*) No, no, I don't mean *leering*, I don't mean *sexual*, I'm talking about mean people in general, just giving *nasty looks*! People around here are such shits. You accidentally bump into one of them on the street— "I'm sorry," you say—and they just *glare* at you. You step in front of somebody to take something off the shelf in a grocery store ... and their eyes just shoot *daggers* through you. You know what I'm talking about? People just seem to be getting nastier and nastier every day. And you know me, I always smile and act humble and excuse myself ... "Pardon me." "I'm sorry." You know. Well, I finally got sick and tired of eating humble pie all the time and I decided to fight back. To fight fire with fire. "The next time somebody's mean to me," I told myself, "I'm gonna be so incredibly mean *back* to them that they are going to shit their pants!" And so I waited ... went through my day, as usual, and waited. Day in, day out ... I waited. I knew that, sooner or later, someone, *somewhere*, would be an asshole and I was ready for 'em. Cut to 2:45 on Thursday. I'm getting on the elevator at work and this guy with a twelve-hundred-dollar-suit is already inside it. Big, fat, really well-groomed, arrogant looking snob. Just me and him. And just as the doors are closing, I open them up again to let this old lady on. Well, you shoulda heard him. He lets out this big GROAN like it's such a fucking hardship that he's gotta wait thirty seconds! So I look at him and sure enough: he's giving me a DIRTY LOOK! So I lay into him. "You selfish son of a bitch," I scream. "You big fat pig! You oughtta be ground up and served as hamburger!" Well, he just about choked on his tongue. He turned *so* red. It was wonderful! That feeling of POWER! I had triumphed over this awful city! This Captain of Industry was withering before my eyes, and it was all because of me! And *then* ... the elevator stopped. On my floor. And the big fat snob gets off with me. He was ... He was our Corporate Supervisor, in from Albany. (*Beat.*) He handed me my pink slip himself. He said, "Enjoy your next *hamburger*." (*Beat.*) But I have to tell you, Marianne ... strange as it sounds? In some deep, dark, primeval way? It was *worth* it.

DO NO WRONG

Ever since I became a celebrity it seems I can do no wrong. No matter what I say, or do ... people *worship* whatever comes out of my mouth! (*Beat.*) The other day, I was doing this television interview ... and they were talking with me about how wholesome I was and how I seemed to have such an ordinary life for being such a big star. And there was this whole crew gathered around me, just gazing at me with these worshipful eyes and open mouths ... *glowing* ... and all of a sudden, my watchband pops and my watch falls off, hits the floor, and shatters. Instinctively, I say "Goddamn, shit!" And I look up and I see that they're all looking at me as if I've just recited words of wisdom! Same thing happened just last night. I was out having dessert with Heather and we were eating chocolate mousse and all of a sudden, I bit into something—like, someone's TOOTH, or something—and it hurt like hell, and I screamed out, "FUCK ME!" And all the people around me just smiled and *applauded*! I was so *livid*, it's like, my private life was their home movie or something. So I picked up my dessert fork and stabbed this blue-haired lady in the hand! AND THEY ALL CHEERED! Bobby, my whole sense of good and bad, right and wrong, moral and immoral, is being turned *upside down*! So to test you, I came in here just now and said I wanted to walk outside stark naked and hail a cab and you said, "Fine." (*Beat.*) WHAT IS GOING ON HERE?

EYE TO EYE

It's really amazing, isn't it? How two people can look at the *same thing* ... and yet come away from it with two totally different perceptions of it. A movie, a painting ... a discussion. A business deal. (*Beat.*) We've usually shared the same taste in movies, Alan. We've usually enjoyed the same painters, the same composers. The same books. But I'm afraid we don't see eye to eye on this business deal. What do you mean, why? How can you *sit* there? You are putting people out on the *street*! Yes you are! It *used* to be a welfare hotel and now where are those people going to go? I doubt they're going to be able to spring for the studio apartments you're going to turn it into. A quarter of a million dollars a throw? (*Beat.*) Of *course* it'll be beautiful. That's hardly the point! You showed me the sketches last year, the blueprints, I told you then, they were beautiful. But I had no idea what the *stakes* were ... Now that I've seen the whole picture, it has grown into something very dark and very ugly. Like Dorian Gray or something. I know, yes, I know, you think I'm being "melodramatic," but that's what this whole thing reminds me of! It's got a very sugary gloss on the outside, a gorgeous exterior ... but on the inside, where nobody really sees, it's cancerous! You cannot justify putting people out on the street in the dead of winter. You *can't* justify it. (*Beat.*) Well then, you're sicker than I thought, because no amount of money is worth what you've turned into. (*Beat.*) You're probably right. There was a time when I *wouldn't* have batted an eye at this. But thank God we don't see eye to eye anymore.

FAITH

If you have enough faith, they say, you can move mountains. Or, something like that. Isn't that in the Bible? I'm not sure. I'm afraid I haven't cracked open a Bible in quite awhile. But my mom used to have this cheesy sampler hanging up in the bathroom with daisies on it and it said on there how faith the size of a mustard seed could move mountains. I saw this magician on some TV show last week and he claimed if you believe, really *believe* in something—anything—you can make it happen. He bent these, ah, these license plates or something to prove his point. You know. Bent them. Without even touching them. From across the room. With his mind. Maybe he was a quack, I don't know. But I have faith, Steven. I do. I have faith in a lot of things: my work, myself ... and even though I haven't known you a long time, I also have a lot of faith in *you*. Now, I don't know what it is with you, maybe you think you *deserve* to be locked up in here, gluing labels on jam jars for the rest of your life. Is that an existence? It's like, you're *hiding*. I don't know what it is, but *some*thing happened to you a long time ago—something awful—and you're still clinging to that. Don't cling, Steven. Don't hang onto it. 'Cause I have faith. I have faith that you can make a new life for yourself. And I don't want you to be scared ... 'cause I have faith ... that somehow, I can help you. And that somehow ... you can begin to help your*self*.

FAKE PLANTS

I bought a dog once. It died. I bought a turtle too, when I was little. With my allowance. It crawled out of its little plastic terrarium thing and we found it petrified under the bed. I also bought a white rat, a goldfish and two hamsters, Myrtle and Josephine. But they all *died*. Plants too. (*Holds up her hand*.) That is *not* a green thumb. Every living thing I come in contact with ... it *dies*! Have you ever looked around my apartment? I mean really taken a good look. Go ahead. Look. Look at the plants. Look at the plants really, really closely. Fake. They're all fake. They may *look* real, but they're fake. I've learned you gotta buy the really expensive ones if you want to promote the illusion of LIVING THINGS. See, I even had fluorescent lights installed above those planters over there so people would *think* they were ALIVE. (*Beat*.) I'm sorry, Stuart. I really am. I feel really torn up inside right now, I really do. But the bottom line is ... I'm a *killer*. And I *can't* say I'll marry you because once I say I'll marry you and I let you into my LIFE ... Well, I'm afraid you'll end up just like Myrtle and Josephine. Dead. And I don't want to have to bury you in the back yard like I did them. Besides. You wouldn't fit inside a matchbox.

71

FIND YOURSELF

I keep looking for that Next Big Thing. (*Beat.*) Shit. I *knew* you'd take it that way! I was not referring to *anything* phallic. I'm talking about *life*, Kay. I'm talking about—. We all exist. We all ... move around, propelled by forces. These forces act on us. Sometimes they're good forces and lift us up and help us to rise above our circumstances. And ... sometimes they're bad forces and they threaten to drag us under. I know all this because a palm reader explained it all to me last night. Madame Zorba. Yeah, well, laugh all you want, but she said something. She said I was looking for The Next Big Thing in my life. I asked her what she meant. "A cause that will fulfill you," she said. "Find your*self* ... and then go find a cause." And I said, "You are worse than those cryptic fortune cookies at Hunan House! What are you talking about?" But she wouldn't tell me. She wouldn't elaborate. I pressed and pressed for an explanation ... but she wouldn't give me one. I was so pissed off. I refused to tip her and I walked out cursing. I mean, who wants *riddles*? I asked for a reading! (*Beat.*) But after I thought about it ... you know, she's right. We never stop to figure out what life's all about. We just drift along, finding bullshit causes to champion. I mean, who *cares* whether the garbage gets picked up twice a week or three times? But that's been our big crusade for weeks now. Fighting the super over an "injustice." I want to find out what makes *me* tick, Kay. Why *I'm* here. Not just when does the garbage go out. (*Beat.*) Yeah, well, go spend a few minutes with Madame Zorba ... and maybe you'll change your mind too.

FIRE WITH FIRE

Is he *smarter* than me? Then what? What, did he go in there and *charm* them? Or—what? He's got more seniority? Like hell he's got seniority, he's been here six months! Do I need to remind you how long I've been here, Thomas? Do I? Three *years.* (*Beat.*) He what? An impression? "He made an impression"? Oh, that's good. That's really good. Smooth. You're so smooth, Thomas. You toss off a line like that and it sounds ... almost *convincing.* But it's only bullshit. *All* your words are bullshit! No, no, I know you don't want to hear this. But you're gonna hear it. Thomas, I've been *killing* myself to get that position! You *know* I have! Coming in here every weekend, staying here weeknights until eight, nine o'clock at night? When they sat in there and discussed this thing, did it ever occur to you to *say* anything in my defense? It didn't, did it? What? It wouldn't have been "appropriate"? Well, that's a new one. After I finished those brochures for you? All those transcripts? This is the thanks I get? (*Beat.*) Well thank you. I'm very glad to know I sound like a shrew. But let me tell you something: if you think this is bad, you just wait. You just wait. You know, I thought we were watching each other's backs. But now I know that you were only watching mine until you could find a chance to stab it. I am *not* "over-dramatizing" things! You *exploited* me! You led me on! You allowed me—you listen to this!—you allowed me to think you were gonna pay me back when the time came! Why else do you think I was breaking my back for you? (*Beat.*) Yeah, well, let me tell you something: you'd better watch *your* back. You hear me, Thomas? 'Cause I'm the kind of person who fights fire with fire.

FIRST STEP

Please. Take it. I can't explain why, I just ... please. I've been doing a lot of thinking and ... I just have to do this. I've been looking at things lately and after what happened to the boy—Jeremy? You remember. (*Beat.*) Well, I did know him. And now I feel ... affected by what happened. So you've just got to trust my judgement and take this. Please. (*Pause.*) I don't expect you to understand this but I'm going to tell you: Jeremy kept this journal. A diary, actually. And after everything calmed down a little, I got to read it. I asked his mother and father for it. I hated doing that because they were just starting to put it all past them at that point and it was like I was opening up the wound all over again. But they agreed. And as I read all his own handwritten notes, a whole new Jeremy began to emerge, to take shape, almost right in front of me. It was a much more vulnerable Jeremy than any of us ever saw in the classroom. An almost desperate Jeremy. In many of his entries, he seemed to be ... *pleading* for something, for—not for sympathy, no, for ... understanding? I'm not sure. (*Beat.*) One thing he wrote in there, he ... he wrote that ... he wished he could really talk to me. *Me.* His teacher! I believe he said, "to share all the things I can only keep to myself." I read that and I realized just how incredibly lonely he was. And I thought, I should have been there for him, why didn't I ever reach out to him? Just once! That's all he wanted. So I tried to reach out to the *other* kids, I tried to talk to *them*—but you keep tying me down with all this goddamn red tape! "You *teach* in the classroom, you don't *talk*," you keep telling me. But what do we end up teaching them? They don't care about the Magna Carta, they want to know, are they *loved*! (*Beat.*) I'm going to start taking time for other people. From now on. I might could've saved that boy's life if I hadn't been so preoccupied. Maybe not, we'll never know. But I have to start somewhere. And this is where I start. So, please. Take my resignation now. Either that, or let *me* decide how to reach these children, my *own* way.

FLATTERY WILL GET YOU KILLED

(*Resentfully.*) Thank you for noticing my new *haircut*, Frank. (*Beat.*) Thanks a lot. I *appreciate* it. (*Beat.*) What? *Yes.* This is a new dress. Thank you. Thanks. Frank. (*Beat.*) Huh? No, no, I already had these earrings. Uh-huh. Look, will you—(*Beat.*) Okay, *look.* Don't even bother to tell me you love my perfume, all right? I *know* your agenda by now. You are so transparent, Frank. It would be repulsive if it wasn't so pathetic! You start with my hair ... move on to my *clothes* ... if it's summer, you remark about my "fabulous tan." Why don't you just COME RIGHT OUT AND TELL ME WHAT IT IS YOU *WANT*! I'd have a *lot* more respect for you that way. Oh, now don't play "innocent" with me! You're always so full of *flattery* for me. Always flirting. Until you get five dollars or a ride home or talk me into swapping shifts with you or WHATEVER IT IS YOU WANT! Then, suddenly, you've lost all interest in me! (*Beat.*) Oh, yeah. Right ... I'll *bet.* You want to take me out? Uh-huh ... (*Beat; SHE realizes he's serious.*) *Really?* (*Apparently so.*) Well. I never thought you had the slightest *interest* in me, Frank, I'm—I'm a bit *surprised* ... Uh-huh. (*Really flattered now.*) Well! I'd like that. I would. Friday? That sounds great! I— what? (*Her smile dissolves into hatred.*) Twenty bucks? You want to borrow TWENTY BUCKS? I KNEW IT! FRANK? YOU ARE A DEAD MAN!

FOOD FIGHT

I can't do it. *Please*, don't ask me again, I just—*I* can't DO it. I can't—. I can't go into that kitchen and prepare a meal with you, because—because you'd be risking your *life*! (*Beat; composes herself, begins.*) My last boyfriend. Let's call him Danny. He was— (*Starting to tear up here.*)—a gourmet chef ... when I first met him, now he can't even cook Minute Rice. That's why I won't go into that kitchen with you! I'M A HAZARD, Alan! I—you don't believe me? Okay then. Here's a little story for you. I'll tell you this little story ... and then you'll know the score. (*Beat.*) Danny found this fantastic-looking recipe for Pressed Liver with Mushroom Paste. They serve it in these tiny little (*SHE indicates.*) portions, it's so rich. Anyway, he spends six *hours* one Saturday preparing this incredible gourmet dish, right? And all he asks me to do is to open the wine. I don't even *like* wine, but I think, well, the least I can do is open it, since he went out and got it. So I'm trying to get the little cork out of the bottle and it won't come and Alan is watching me and he can't *believe* that I can't do a simple little thing like opening a bottle, so he reaches over to help me and at that INSTANT—the cork goes shooting out of the bottle and hits the little neon light in the ceiling. You know, those cute little circular ones? And it shatters and these sparks come shooting out, and they land on the paper towel roll. And that gets set on fire. He's screaming to throw it in the sink, but I don't want to grab it 'cause it's on *fire*! So I try to knock it into the sink with a ladle but I catch the potholders on fire—see, we had all these potholders hanging up by the sink too—and before we know it, the fire alarm goes off and the whole kitchen is in flames. Then I remember hearing somewhere that you could *beat* a fire out with a skillet. So I grab this big metal skillet but before I have a chance to get to the fire—I hit Danny in the head. Knock him unconscious. The Fire Department came. Gave Danny mouth-to-mouth 'til he came around. But he swore he would never, ever prepare a meal with me again. And since our whole relationship was sort of, well, *based* on food ... that was the beginning of the end for us. Oh, we tried to live on fast food for awhile. Pizza. Frozen dinners. Take-out. But the passion was gone. He moved out within the month. (*Beat.*) Now you see why I won't go in there with you. I love you so, so very much. And to walk in there and bake a *cake* with you ... might be the end of *us*. (*Beat.*) What? You'll do it *alone*? (*Tearing up again, happily.*) Oh ... I love you!

FRESH MEAT

Remember when you first started working here? We started at about the same time. The way everybody treated us? (*Laughs*.) They were so *awful*! So *cynical* ... they called us "fresh meat." If you were fresh meat, they could do anything to you! Kirk used to insult me in front of everybody—remember? Almost daily!—and you were subjected to all those ridiculous "errands" all the time. But we put up with it. We never complained. I guess we were pretty naive back then. (*Beat*.) Do you realize how long we've been here? Four years. Yeah, four years, next month. And you know what? Now *we're* the cynical ones. Have you noticed? Ever since all those new applications started coming in, *we're* the ones who've been joking around about "When are we gonna get some 'fresh meat' in this place?" (*Beat*.) We've changed, Marsha. We have! We used to be so ... innocent, and we're not like that at all anymore. And it kind of *scares* me. I always *swore* I'd never be like "them" ... and just look at me: that's exactly what I've turned into. (*Beat*.) I'm not making fun of them anymore, Marsha. I won't do it. You want to treat them like "fresh meat," you go right ahead. You can give them all the attitude you want. But I am going to give them my respect. After all, that's what we thought *we* deserved, didn't we?

HIDDEN

I am *trying* to understand this, Doug. I really am. But it's ... hard.
You and I are different in *so many ways*. (*Beat.*) Yeah, well, at first
it was fun. It was invigorating. It was a challenge. But now ... it's
really become a pain in the ass. I know we're products of different
backgrounds and all: you were taught that drinking was wrong; as a
child I was given *wine* at the dinner table—you don't like to talk
about your feelings, I *do*—I know all that. But it's like, there are
parts of you that are just ... *hidden* from me, and when they come to
the surface, I'm just—shocked! (*Beat.*) I always knew you didn't like
Lisa. I could tell. I just didn't realize it was because she's black—
no, it's TRUE! IT'S TRUE! You like *all* my other friends but
you've never had anything nice to say about Lisa and she's the
sweetest person I know. I never put it all together until now, but
now I see: whenever she calls, you "forget" to give me the message.
Whenever I make plans for the three of us to have dinner or
something, you have to "work late" at the last moment. And now
this! When I told Mom I wanted her to be my bridesmaid, you had a
fucking FIT! No, you *did,* and I'm mad, Doug! I'm mad as *hell* right
now! You what? You don't want to talk about it? Okay, fine. *Don't*
talk. But *I* don't mind talking, and I'll tell you something: it's *not*
too late to call this whole thing off. (*Beat.*) Well, maybe that's what
we should do. 'Cause I'm not sure I want to go through with it. All
of a sudden, I don't think I know who you really are ... and before
we tie that knot, I want to make sure you're someone I can believe
in, not a hidden hypocrite.

HOPE

If you were to die, would you be missed? I don't mean by your mother and father, 'cause of *course* they'd be hysterical, that's a given. But other people I mean. Would the people you've known really miss you? *(Beat.)* I was thinking last night ... and I came to the conclusion that if I were to kill myself ... I really don't think anybody would care. No, no, I'm not trying to manipulate you, I'm not, 'cause I know how much you hate being manipulated! You tell me, like, *all* the time. I'm just saying. *(Beat.)* I went to the Duane Reade last night to buy some Kleenex and toilet paper and stuff and when I got home and unpacked everything, I realized that I had bought a bottle of sleeping pills. And I sat there for half an hour looking at that bottle of little white pills, wondering what would happen if I just washed all of them down with a glass of tap water. You'd be upset. My mother would throw herself on *my* coffin, or some damn thing. But who else would be affected? I'll tell you: Nobody. Life would go on for the rest of the ten trillion people on this planet like I never even existed. *(Beat.)* Where's that hope, Brian? That sense of hope we had when we were children? We always felt comforted, always felt ... protected. What happens to that when we grow up? I swear, I don't know whatever happened to that side of me. But if I don't find it again ... I am gonna be in whole lot of trouble.

HUMAN ICICLES

It is *so cold* in here! (*Beat.*) I mean it! I am not kidding! It is so cold ... (*Beat.*) I don't think I have ever been this cold in my *life* before! Have *you*? Oh, well, sure. You're from Minnesota, you're probably used to walking around in blizzards in your underwear or something. But I'm from Arizona. We're not *used* to this. We're not! (*Beat; SHE shivers, then gets an idea.*) Stomp your feet! Somebody told me once, that gets the blood going. (*SHE does so for quite a while; SHE stops; looks disheartened.*) It doesn't work, does it? Oh, God. I hope we don't freeze to death in here. What if that happened? What if we really and truly *froze* to death and they found, like, these two huge human icicles in the morning? What would your obituary say? I know what *mine* would say: "Angela McMullen. She lived and she died. Period." Nothing in between. (*SHE starts to cry.*) If I ever get out of here *alive*, I am going to *do* something with my life! I will! I *swear* I will! I'm gonna live out all my dreams! I'm gonna travel to all the places I always wanted to go! I'm gonna do all the crazy things I always wanted to do! *You'll* see! I'm gonna make absolutely certain that the next time the *heat* goes off like this ... I will be prepared for death!

81

I LOVE ANIMALS

I love animals. And I don't mean that as a generalization, either. I really *love* them. Love to hold them. Love to take care of them. Love to *own* them! I have five cats, a hamster, one parakeet and a monkey. He broke both of those lamps, naughty boy. (*Calling off.*) Elroy, you're a naughty boy! (*Back to the subject.*) We saw this horse last weekend when we went upstate and I wanted it too, but Jeffrey said no. Jeffrey's kind of a poop about animals. He doesn't love animals like *I* do. He loves *me*, I know that, but he definitely has a problem with animals. He says we have a two-bedroom apartment and that if I bring any more animals home, he's going to pack up and leave on the next train home to Richmond. (*Beat.*) Okay. So here's the deal: I found this *adorable* German Shepherd today ... and it's homeless! Did you see him? I named him Spike. He's in the bathroom. Well, I just *had* to take him in! I know, I know what Jeffrey said, I know. If I bring one more animal in, he's gonna leave. So I made out one of those pro and con lists. You know, the advantages of having Jeffrey and the disadvantages of having Jeffrey. He is a great guy ... and he does pay half the rent ... but on the other hand he complains a lot and I know he's not gonna wanna walk Spike. See? I kept coming up with lots of reasons like that, and when I had finished, both of my lists had pretty much come out even. I ended up with just as many reasons to *keep* Jeffrey as I did to get *rid* of him! (*Beat.*) *You* know Jeffrey pretty well, Alan. I'd say you're his best friend. How do *you* think I ought to handle the situation? I mean, I *want* Jeffrey ... but I *also* want Spike and Elroy and all the rest of my animals. And a horse one day! Do you think there is some way that I could possibly have all of them? (*SHE waits for an answer.*) Take your time. Think about it. He won't be home for at least another ... (*Checks her watch.*) ... five minutes.

I'M NOT STUPID

I'M NOT STUPID, AM I? I'm NOT! Whenever we have a conversation, I have pretty intelligent things to contribute, don't I? *I* think so. Like last night, when you were saying that the economy was in rigor mortis, I provided you with a wonderfully candid assessment of the many other failing global economies: the Third World, Russia, the Middle East ... and I offered up a ten-minute study on the growing impact of Japanese trade on the United States Marketplace. (*Beat.*) So then why do I *choke* on my tongue whenever I'm around my boss? Or any other authority figure? I feel like a ten-year-old whenever I go in there. He asks me the *simplest* thing: "Miss Graham, when is President's Day?" or "Miss Graham, where is the Sports Section?" And I *choke*! I gag on my words as if they were tainted peach cobbler! "Afksazzdt," I say. "Mfftragh!" *WHY*? Why *is* that? What is it inside us that causes us to *dry up* in the presence of those who are considered to be our "superiors?" I *hate* it. I really do. It's been a curse all my *life* and I am *not* going to take it anymore! I am not going to stand there in the presence of my boss, my doctor, my father-in-law ... and stumble all over my words! I am a *valuable person*, and I *recognize* that! So. I have decided to face this problem the right way. By *dealing* with it. No more hiding from people I'm scared of. No more stammering all over myself when I'm asked what time it is. NO MORE! (*Beat.*) What am I gonna *do*? I'm gonna learn *sign language*! That's the only reasonable solution, don't you think?

LOSS

"Cheer up." How in hell do you expect me to do that? Huh? Look, it's not that I don't want your advice; I just don't *want* your advice, Anna! Your advice is *worthless*. When there's a hole this big inside you—you never fill it up again. Nothing can fill that hole, nothing can take the place of what's missing. You don't just "cheer up." It doesn't happen. Part of you's gone and you remember that every moment you're awake. And asleep, too. Do you have any idea the *nightmares* I still have? (*Beat.*) People keep telling me—especially Mom and Dad—"It's okay. You'll get over it with *time*. Time heals everything." Well, let me tell you something: Those are just cliched lyrics to bad pop songs. Time heals nothing. The loss, the *wanting*, is just as painful as it was one week before, one month before, one year before. The bottom line is, you gotta go through it alone. No matter how many people are "with you," "around you," you're still facing it alone. (*Beat.*) It's Jenny's birthday, Anna. She would've been two years old if she were still ... alive. But she's not. She's gone. Sure, Philip and I can adopt, sure we can, everybody keeps telling me that over and over again, but that doesn't bring Jenny back! My Jenny is gone forever. *That's* the cold, hard truth. I will never be able to hold her again. No matter how much I *want* to ... (*Beat.*) I have to live with that. You don't have to. Mom doesn't have to. Dad doesn't have to. *I* have to. So don't tell me to cheer up. I'd only be doing it for you.

MAKING IT

How will we know? When we "get there," I mean? We always used to talk about how we wanted to "make it." Have we "made it" yet? Or are we still trying? I honest-to-God don't know anymore, Ellen. Ten years ago—*five* years ago—if someone told me I'd be doing what I'm doing now, getting paid what I'm getting paid now ... I'd have said, "hot damn!" I'd have thought that I was "making it." But here I am ... and it's just not *enough*. This is such a cutthroat business. And I just keep wondering, will I ever be *secure*? *Ever*? (*Beat.*) God knows we've made sacrifices, Ellen. I could've taken that sales job in Denver. Or the retail thing in Indianapolis. Those would've been easy and I'd probably be married by now. Kids. A great house. But ... *career* came first. (*Beat.*) I've watched all our friends: Susan. Linda. Marjorie ... One by one, they've fallen by the wayside. One by one, they've gotten married or found something else to *do* with their lives. And I know we used to criticize them for that, but when I see them, when I talk to them ... they *seem happy*. I think they're happy. Do you think they're happy? (*Beat.*) But here *we* are. We keep right on trying to climb that ladder. All of a sudden, I'm asking myself, "What in the hell are we working towards?" I don't *know* anymore. And even if I *did* know, when we *get* there ... you gotta ask yourself, "Is this worth it?" (*Beat.*) Well, is it? You tell me.

MAN IN THE SHOEBOX

My father was *great*. At least, the father I *invented* was great. Loving. Patient. Kind ... (*Beat.*) See, I never *knew* my father. He left us when I was two. Took off. Mom says he just disappeared one night and never came back. (*Beat.*) For the longest time, I didn't even know what he looked like! I mean, for *years*! Mom threw all his pictures away. Or so I thought. Then, one day, Mom's at work and I'm in her room playing dress up. You know. evening gown four sizes too big for me; her shoes, pearls, the works. And I notice this old shoebox under her bed. I was always a curious kid. So, I take it out ... and it's full of old pictures. Photographs. Snapshots. Of Dad and Mom, together. From years before. This whole box just filled with old pictures. Some of them faded ... some of them torn in half ... (*Beat.*) Many times over the next few years, I'd sneak in there and empty that box out. Pour all those snapshots out on the floor. Study his face ... He had such a kind face. I couldn't understand. Why a man with such a kind face ... would leave his family. (*Beat.*) As time went on, I created a whole personality for that man in the shoebox. I had no idea who he *really* was ... so I could afford to make him the most wonderful man in the world. I made him what I wanted. I created my own father. I made up birthday parties that he had never thrown for me ... I made up bedtime stories that he had never read to me. I made up *everything*. (*Beat.*) But then, one day I went in there ... and she had thrown them out. All the pictures. Gone. (*Beat.*) I know, it sounds like your dad is a real bastard. But at least he's *here* ... *Talk* to him. Maybe it's not too late to work this out. At least it's a chance, Carol. A chance I never got.

ME IN A NUTSHELL

It's really simple, Leonard: People *terrify* me. I'm not even talking about the dangerous element that's lurking out there—murderers, rapists, criminals—I'm just talking about average people. You've heard of stage fright? Call mine life fright; I don't know what it is or where it stems from. But the act of sitting down and conversing with a stranger ... that to me is more terrifying than walking down 12th Avenue after midnight. That probably sounds weird to somebody so outgoing like you, but there it is. That's me in a nutshell. That's why you had to call me thirteen times before I'd agree to talk to you. And why we had to talk on the phone six times before I'd agree to go out with you. I've been really, really *brave*. Aren't you proud of me? I went out to the movies with you and the opera and last week we went ICE-SKATING—can you believe it? ICE-SKATING—ME! And here we are, we're going along fine, we're getting along and everything ... and all of a sudden you go and ask me to *marry* you? What are you trying to *do*? Send me all the way back to SQUARE ONE?

MEDICINE

Maybe I'm just an alarmist. That's what my husband calls me. And, God, I *hope* that's all it is. But I just hopped on a plane and flew all the way here from Idaho so I *want* an answer! (*Beat.*) Did you look in that plastic bag? Take a look. Look inside that plastic bag and tell me what you see. (*Beat.*) Good. Medicine. That's right, Doctor. Medicine. Prescription bottles. Do you have any *idea* how many prescription bottles are in that plastic bag? I'll tell you: twenty-six. Twenty-six *different* bottles of medicine. And do you know whose *name* is on each and every one of those bottles? My *father*. No, no—I'm not accusing you of *anything*, I just want to know, I want to—WAIT A MINUTE! (*Beat.*) I am very grateful to you for looking after Dad. I have to tell you that. Fred's work has taken him out to the Midwest—yeah, well, you know all that. You know we would've stayed here if it weren't for that and we are very grateful for all you've done. But ... well, Dad seems like he was doing better *before*. Before he was taking all this stuff. All of a sudden, we come home and—and he's so *lethargic*, so *slow*, and yes, I *know* he's getting old, but it's like he's a different person now and it *scares* me! (*Beat.*) Is it *safe* for somebody to be taking all this medication *every day*? I mean, come on, Dr. Randall, we're talking about twenty-six different pills *every single day*! (*Beat.*) Do you even *know* what each of these pills does? (*Beat.*) You *do*. Well, then, you're going to tell me. Yes, you are. We are going to dump each and every one of these bottles out on the counter and you are going to tell me *why* each of these drugs has been administered. Because if you *can't* ... then something has got to be done.

NEVER LOOK BACK

Of *course* I've thought about them! All I've been able to think about is them! But who's thinking about *me*? Ten thousand dollars. Is that supposed to make all the pain go away? Her birth ... was the most beautiful thing that has ever *happened* to me. How can you put a price on that? I know, I know I signed a contract, I know I've taken the money. But I'll give the money back! I'll tear up the contract! I'll do anything, but I won't give up this baby! (*Beat.*) Everybody's so worried about them. "How are *they* going to feel? How will they react? They've been waiting *so long* for a baby." Well, who's been *carrying* her for the last nine months? Does anybody care about me? Did anybody ever ask how *I* feel? THIS IS MY BABY! Just because we all signed a few pieces of paper and a check changed hands ... that doesn't fix how you *feel*! She's mine! I have loved her and taken care of her and talked to her and dreamed about what she'll be when she grows up, what she'll look like, where she'll live, will they be good to her ... what, now I'm supposed to just hand her over and never look back? You get them on the phone and you tell them the whole thing's off. I don't want to hurt them. That's not what I want here. I just love my baby and *I* want to take care of her.

NEW YEAR'S DAY

I'd pretty much put it out of my mind. Buried it. I *thought*. But it always comes back around the holidays. See, there's kind of a lot of guilt in something like this. It wasn't my *fault,* but still ... something like that happens and you don't *think* clearly, you don't *act* quickly enough! What is it they say? "Hindsight is 20-20?" And that's true. I mean, if I could go back ... if I could just go back and do it all *over* again ... Well, I'd like to *think* I'd do something different. I'd like to *think* so. But maybe I wouldn't. I don't know. It all boils down to one thing: in that situation, it was me or her. Me or her. And I *let* it be her. That's why we're not that ... big ... on New Year's Eve anymore, Eric. (*Beat.*) On New Year's Eve, three years ago, Martha and I ... we were coming out of this club— New Year's *Day,* I mean, it was, like, three in the morning—and we were the last ones outta this place. We came out into this empty parking lot ... and this guy, this guy was waiting outside. Leaning up against Martha's car. We made a joke about, "Lost your car?" or something like that ... But he wasn't laughing. And as we got closer to the car ... he wouldn't move. He ... he had a gun. And he—(*Beat.*) Well, let's put it this way: I ran. And my sister didn't run fast enough. (*Beat.*) It took me fifteen minutes to find a cop. And by then he was ... (*Beat.*) finished with her. (*Beat.*) Martha and I still haven't ... *dealt* with it. Not totally. I mean, we're still close and everything but there's this chasm between us now, this dark place because we haven't really *talked* about why I was spared and she was ... sacrificed. So now you see why we're not that big on New Year's. (*Beat.*) Maybe I did the right thing. I don't know, maybe not. But that's not good enough for me, in my own mind. Because that's a question that will never be answered. The only thing I know for sure is that, sometimes ... like right *now* ... I wish it had been me.

NEW PERSPECTIVE

When I was a little girl, my Grandmother made me this sweater with Snoopy on it. Hand-knitted, you know, she picked out the yarn herself and made this sweater from scratch. It was pink and had Snoopy asleep on his doghouse and it was my favorite sweater and I wore it just about all the time. I came across it the last time we moved and you know me, I'm not very sentimental, I tossed it into a big trash bag with the rest of my rags and had Bill take it all to the dump. Somebody said we ought to give all our old clothes to Goodwill, but it was just too much trouble, we decided just to throw it all out. We must've filled up six or seven *big* trash bags—those big lawn bags?—with old clothes. This was, like, last May, right? Well, just a couple of weeks ago, I'm leaving work, right, and I'm standing there on 9th Avenue, trying to catch a cab, and it was positively *freezing* out. I was blowing on my hands to try and keep warm, and for some reason, I glanced up and saw this homeless man huddled in a doorway. Curled up all in a ball trying to stay warm. He had some of those plastic rain boots on—you know, the kind children wear?—a pair of sweat pants with holes all in them ... and my Snoopy sweater. He was *wearing* that old pink Snoopy sweater that I threw out in the trash. I gave him everything I had in my wallet. Twenty-eight dollars and three subway tokens. And instead of a cab, I walked home that night. (*Beat.*) I have always felt ... insulated, from the problems we're always hearing about on the news. But seeing that man ... it brought it right home to me and slapped me in the face. (*Beat.*) I will *never* walk past someone in need again, Debbie. I don't know exactly what I'll do ... but I will *not* just walk on by. Not anymore.

NICE LITTLE TOUCHES

Are you happy with me? I mean, are you *happy*? I don't know, just—well, there was a time when I wouldn't have to ask you to hold the door for me. What do you mean, "When was that?" When we first started dating! You used to do a lot of chivalrous things back then. You took me out on fancy dates ... dancing ... made sure you walked me to my door every time you took me home ... opened the car door for me ... asked if it was all right if you watched the ball game. Now you just *watch* it. I know, I sound like I'm complaining. I'm not complaining. I *hate* complaining. I hate *people* who complain. Maybe I'm just having a bad day, I dunno. Maybe ... (*Stops herself, then.*) I found that old scrapbook this afternoon while you were watching the ball game. Pictures of us. When we first started going out? And you are smiling in every one of them. Big ol' smile! Like you were so happy just to be alive. So grateful. And I realized ... you don't smile like that anymore. Well, if you do, I don't notice. I just thought, maybe you've gotten bored with me, or you wish you'd married someone else or something. I know people get familiar with each other. That just happens. It's a natural part of relationships and it's true, those "nice little touches" do kind of fall by the wayside after awhile. I guess I just miss getting flowers and going on *dates*, and—what? Tomorrow night? (*Beat; SHE smiles.*) I thought you'd never ask!!

NO THREAT

Janet? No, thank you, really. The Jello salad was wonderful, but I'm full. Really. Listen, I wanted to talk to you, because—no, no more coffee, thanks. One more bite or sip of anything and I swear I'll pop! I'm fine. I just thought maybe we should talk, because, you know, since you've come to live with—the what? The recipe? Sure, I'll take it, if you insist, but—Janet! *Look*! Will you sit *down*? Just sit down and be still for, like, five minutes and just *talk* to me! (*Beat.*) I'm sorry. I don't mean to sound pissy. You've done a lot for me since you've come here. I appreciate that. And I *really* appreciate the way you've taken care of Daddy and—well, I know. I'm glad you found each other. I never thought Daddy would marry again, his standards were always so high for Mom and me and after he and Mom got divorced ... well, I'm just glad he found you. But I feel like, all of a sudden, it's like you and I are competing for the same prize. Like, you feel I'm going to ally myself with Mom somehow and try to throw you over or something. No, no it's *not* just my imagination! Sometimes we're all sitting in the same room together, and it's like I have to fight you just to get his attention! Just to ask him how his week was! You practically kill yourself to keep him busy, you make all these big fancy meals ... Janet, *listen* to me: I am NO THREAT! You don't have to "win" him away from Mom. Or away from me. I think you're great and I'm glad he has you. And Mom, well ... she's finding her own life now. (*Beat.*) Janet, you don't have to *try* so hard. You've already got my blessing. And you know you have his love. There's nothing else you need to fight for.

OBJECT

I am so sick of being looked at as an object! (*Snaps fingers repeatedly, as if trying to wake someone from a daze.*) Do you understand what I'm saying? Do my words register at all in that hollow head of yours? I really wanted to have a nice time tonight. I really did. A nice dinner ... nice conversation ... But I have barely been able to swallow ONE BITE of this meal or concentrate on ONE WORD you've said because YOU HAVE BEEN STARING AT MY CHEST ALL NIGHT LONG! (*Beat.*) I'm so miserable. I could just throw up right about now. Just stick my finger down my throat and VOMIT all over this white lace tablecloth. I wonder if you'd be ogling me then? Huh? If I really did something disgusting like that? Or if I popped out a fake eyeball and dropped it in my wine glass and laughed like a SAILOR? Sometimes I wish I could do something like that. Something just so vile and disgusting that it'd break this—this SPELL I seem to cast on men. I mean, look at you! You're a nice guy. I was looking forward to spending some time with you. But the moment you showed up at my apartment door, you set your sights on THESE (*Her chest.*) and you haven't once lifted them to look me STRAIGHT IN THE EYE! (*Beat.*) There. That's better. (*A warning.*) Ah-ah. Keep 'em up here. Soon as I see 'em drift down there again ... this swordfish comes back up. Right in your LAP!

PEOPLE LIKE YOU

There's a *name* for people like you. You hear me? People like you, you think ... Yeah, well, there's a *name* for that. For that kind of behavior. That kind of sick thinking. You know what you are? You're a *bloodsucker*. (*Beat.*) Look, I was in here *last* week. And a bottle of olives was $2.49. I come back today to pick up a couple more bottles for this cocktail party we're having ... and suddenly they're $2.*89*! What, suddenly there's a vast shortage of OLIVES in the world? The price was suddenly driven UPward? The olive growers of the world have united in some grand plot to hold up production so that capitalists like ourselves will suffer? I think not. I think not. What I think, what is most *likely* ... is that you're just some slimy little worm who's taking advantage of working people like *me*! And him! And her! We break our backs to earn our puny little wages ... we haul our weary carcasses in here to plunk down our miserable savings on a few measly GROCERIES! And what do you do? You raise the *prices*! Every week, things just keep creeping upward and upward. Oh sure, sometimes it's just a nickel or a dime ... but it all adds up. No, you let me FINISH! Someone has to put a stop to this! Someone has to say "no, not anymore!" And that someone is *me*! I am *not* paying an extra forty cents so that you can profit from *my* misfortune! I will not contribute to your bloodsucking, criminal lifestyle! I would rather walk the fifteen blocks I'm going to have to walk ... in the blistering cold ... to the Food Court, halfway across town ... and buy *their* friggin' olives! I'd rather do that than be taken advantage of by you! And I know your store doesn't have a long line, but I'd rather wait in Food Court's line for an hour and a half to save the forty cents you're robbing me of! I'd rather ... (*Beat.*) Shit. Who am I kidding? I'm gonna walk all the way over there just to save forty *cents*? Forget it. Forget I said anything. Here. I'll take *three*.

PERFECT FANTASY MAN

I took one of those magazine quiz things today. You know, where you answer all those "yes or no" questions? I know, they're silly, but they're *fun*. Anyway, listen. The name of this quiz was "Who Is Your Perfect Fantasy Man?" And the questions were all designed to make you forget every detail about whoever you were married to or lived with or whatever. They were designed to block him out of your mind and to get you to be objective and make you clearly realize *what* your true fantasy man would be like. So I took out a Number 2 and went to work. Circled all my yes's. All my no's. Tallied up all the answers. And do you know what? This is so funny! My perfect fantasy man could *not* have been more different from you! It said my ideal mate was the exact opposite of you in every way! But you know what? I'll tell you something ... *You* are my perfect fantasy man. You are! I never stopped to realize that before. I think we kind of take each other for granted sometimes. I mean, look at us: we're so busy and everything, always running around ... But I just wanted you to know that. That you're my perfect fantasy man. You glad? Good. *(Beat; then a sly smile.)* Am I your perfect fantasy *woman*?

PRIDE

I used to clean house for Miz Rawlins. You know that woman. Her husband's the foot doctor. Them folks had so much money they didn't know what to *do* with it! Couldn't a spent all of it if they'd tried to. (*Beat.*) She paid me three dollars an hour, the whole time I worked for her. And this was three, four years. Some days I'd come in to work as early as six in the morning. Work 'til after dark. Down on my knees, washing her kitchen floor 'til it just *shined*. I did good work for her. And still, up to the very end, three dollars an hour. (*Beat.*) One day, I decided I had to stand up for myself. I told her I needed a raise. She asked me what I thought was fair. I said four dollars an hour. She didn't say nothing. Next day I went in there, she had all these *things* laid out on the bed. She was gonna give 'em to me. She said here you are Emma, I'm gonna give you these. Some old raggedy-lookin' hat her *momma* must've worn ... blue jeans that she had outgrown ... two sweaters that had stains all over 'em. Just junk, really. That's all it was, was junk. Not even fit to give to the second hand store. I asked her, was this in addition to that raise I'd asked for? But I already knew what she was gonna say ... It was in *place* a that raise. (*Beat.*) I told her I was sorry, but that I couldn't work for her no more. On my way out the door, she offered me three and a quarter, I heard her calling to me ... but I just kept right on walking. (*Beat.*) Sometimes you gotta be practical, I *know* that honey. But sometimes ... you gotta keep your pride.

READY TO ACT

My father always told me it was wrong to hate people. But I sure hate that son of a bitch Greg. Don't you? The way he walks around the office. Nose up in the air. Monday, day I wore my new outfit? He walked up to my desk and looked down at me and said—in that whiny little nasal voice he has—"Hmm. Sale at Kress last Saturday?" He's always doing stuff like that to me. Jana, too. Insulting us? Making fun of us? Last week, he made some crack about Jana's boobs. I don't know, he asked if he could set his ashtray down for awhile or something. I know they're enormous, but what right does he have? In front of everybody? Ugh! Don't you just hate him? I do. (*Beat.*) Oh, don't give me all that karma crap again. Just because you hate somebody doesn't mean something bad's gonna happen to you. Yeah, right. Because I hate this guy, I'm gonna get hit by a bus or something. Right? Yeah, right. Why doesn't anything awful happen to *him*? He's a constant pain in *everybody*'s ass. Well, I don't care what you say. I hate him and I am going to do something about it. Next time he gets within two feet of me ... I'm going to pick this stapler up and nail him right between the legs! And maybe I will get paid back by your karma or whatever it is, okay, fine. But at least I'll know that I put a staple where it counts. That's putting your money where your mouth is, Susan. And I'm ready to act.

SELF-ESTEEM

He did *not* wink at me. He had something in his *eye*. *(Beat.)* I don't
know. Dust, or dirt, or a torn contact lens, how should *I* know? But
it was *not* a wink. *This* is a wink. *(Demonstrates.)* What he did was
more like this—*(Demonstrates.)*—like, a nervous tic, or—STOP
IT! Okay? Look, guys don't wink at me! I don't know, I'm just not
the kind of girl that guys stop and stare at. I'm not like *you. (Beat.)*
Well, I'm sorry if I sound "pointed," but you keep going on and on
about how *beautiful* I am. I've got a mirror. I know what I look
like. Oh, now don't start with that again. All your talk about "low
self-esteem." My self-esteem is *fine.* There is nothing wrong with
my self-esteem. Just—well, maybe *you* ought to try going places
with you sometimes. Like at O'Grady's the other night. When we
stopped by for a couple of drinks? I swear, you're like some kind of
... MAN-MAGNET. They all swarm around you like ants. Pretend
I'm not there. And you're so busy enjoying it all—well, who
wouldn't enjoy it—that you never even see what I'm going through.
You and all your "suitors" just forget all about me. *(Beat.)* I never
told you about this, but remember that time Danny Sullivan asked
me out? Yeah. Well, I know I said I had a great time, but ... I lied.
All he did the whole night was ask about *you.* All night long. I
finally pretended I was sick and asked him to take me home. I ran
upstairs and cried my damn eyes out. I'm not trying to make you
feel awful. I just want you to *see* ... it's more complicated than self-
esteem. It's complicated ... because I want us to stay friends. And,
sometimes, I—*(Beat; SHE sees something off in the distance, tries
to continue.)* Sometimes, I—*(Sees it again.)* Oh, my God! You're
right! He *is* winking at me! Oh my God! He's coming *over* here!
OH MY GOD! Quick! What do I *say* to him?

SEX APPEAL

When I was little, we were so poor I couldn't afford to take my lunch to school. If I didn't get up in time to eat breakfast, I just went hungry all day. S'all there was to it. My stomach'd growl so loud in math class that everybody'd turn their heads and look at me. Stare at me. I was so ashamed. But then I discovered I had something—I had a commodity—and that I could use it to get me what I wanted. I had sex appeal. (*Beat.*) I learned to look at the little boys until they blushed and turned away. I learned how to talk ... real soft, like. So that my voice'd get inside their heads and gnaw at their little brains. By the time I was in 7th grade, I had half the boys in my class lined up, offering me their lunches. In exchange for a kiss. They got to where they'd compete. Who could bring the best lunch, that kind of thing. After a year or two of that, I filled-out. I wasn't so scrawny anymore. And I had sharpened my one asset into a well-defined tool. Like I said, we didn't have much. But I learned to do a lot with a little. I learned how to dress to my advantage. I guess nowadays kids'd call me white trash. But when you've never had anything in your life and suddenly you're the center of attention ... well, you couldn't care less what other kids think. (*Beat.*) Trading lunches for kisses sort of ... escalated. Into other things. More serious things. I didn't realize what was happening at the time, things were ... they were moving pretty fast. I had to keep topping myself to keep 'em interested. (*Beat.*) Yeah. I had sex appeal. But where did it get me? At sixteen I was single, pregnant, and *still* dirt poor. (*Beat.*) Trust me. From someone who *knows*. Sex appeal may seem like a real asset, honey. But you gotta control *it*. 'Cause once it starts to control *you* ... you're in big trouble.

SKI MASKS

We always thought that buying a house in this day and age would be impossible. I mean, my parents paid $10,000 for their first house. The little one in Concord? Yeah. But you can't even get a good *car* for that nowadays. When we started looking at houses last year, we couldn't believe it! $350,000! $400,000! Oh, it's awful! Besides, Jeffrey only makes $27,000 a year teaching. So ... (*Beat*). We robbed a bank. (*Beat*.) No, no I'm serious. We—no, really. First Olympian Savings and Loan. Yeah. We went to K-Mart and bought a couple of ski-masks ... Jeffrey confiscated some kid's B-B-Gun at school, this really convincing-looking rifle ... and we robbed the bank. Don't you remember? It was in the papers and everything. Last fall. Yes, yes, that was us! (*SHE's proud of her accomplishment*.) Obviously we *weren't* arrested, or I wouldn't be sitting here telling you all this, would I? The police never had any clue that—Ellen! Ellen, wait! Hold on now, I'm not—Ellen! Listen to me! DON'T GET HYSTERICAL! (*Beat*.) I am *not* a criminal. I am your *friend*. And I only told you this to *help*. I mean, you said Bill couldn't afford a down payment, *so* ... (*Raises her eyebrows*.) Oh, come on, Ellen! *Everybody* steals. It's all relative! You probably swipe staplers and calculators from your office, right? (*Beat*.) Paper? (*Beat*.) Paper *clips*? (*Beat*.) *Nothing*? (*Beat*.) Boy, you really *are* a Polly Purebread, aren't you? (*Beat*.) Well, it all boils down to *one thing*: How badly do you *want* a house?—Now don't! Don't answer right now. Take your time. And *think* about it. And before you make up your mind, just imagine what it'll be like with two kids in this apartment. This tiny box with no windows. Even one child. Screaming. Day in and day out. (*Screams like a baby, then:*) It's not very appealing, is it? Mm-hmm ... Well, you think it over. But if you decide you need a couple of ski masks and a B-B-Gun ... you know who to come to.

SLAVE TO SICKNESS

I've had a perpetual cold since I was two years old. Snotty, runny nose. Watery eyes. Puffy little face. You know. My entire childhood was spent in the waiting rooms of every doctor's office within a ninety-mile radius of our home. Searching. My mother was constantly searching for The Cure. At first, they thought it was allergies. So they spent months and months testing me to see what things I was allergic to. Pricking me with little needles to see if my skin would break out. And the funny thing is, that no matter what doctor we went to, he or she would find that the cause was something else! One doctor would determine that it was chocolate. So I couldn't eat candy bars. But after weeks of not eating candy bars, I still wasn't better so they took me to another specialist. And she said, no it's fish. She's allergic to any kind of fish. So then I couldn't eat fish. Or butter. Or fried foods, you name it and someone decided that it made me sick. Even Jello! Can you believe it? I got so tired of being ill all the time. I was a slave to sickness. But do you realize? Look at me. I'm not sick *now*! All my life, I've been searching for the thing-that-will-make-me-well-again, and all of a sudden, as soon as I stopped trying so hard, I'm okay. Why am I telling you all this? I know that's what you're thinking. I'm telling you all this because I have you to thank. Ever since we met, you've kept me so happy ... like I've never been before. And by concentrating on being happy—instead of being so *paranoid* that everything I come in contact with is going to make me *sick* ... I suddenly realized, I haven't been sick for *months*! I know it sounds weird, but it's true. Now just accept the compliment and let's dig into these candy bars! It'll be my first one in about fifteen years.

SPONTANEITY

I wish I was as witty as you are. No, I mean it. I wish I could come up with jokes like you. How do you get that way? I guess you read a lot, huh? Books. The newspapers. I had a feeling about you, Brian. I don't know. But I just had this feeling ... *(Beat.)* Is that why I never see you out with the rest of the office? I mean, when they all go out to party? You're sitting at home, making up jokes, eh? Hey, hey, look. Don't get insulted! I'm not trying to *insult* you ... I just—*(Beat.)* I see a sadness in you, Brian. The same sadness I used to see in myself. I think I used to be a lot like you. I used to worry so much about what people *thought* of me. I practiced what I was gonna say, how I was gonna say it. Stayed up late watching the news so I could get in on the coffee klatch. Spontaneity was my greatest fear. I avoided every spontaneous gathering for fear that I'd go out with everybody, *unprepared,* and say something *stupid.* I don't know what I was so scared of. That they wouldn't *like* me anymore? I don't know. I *do* know that, once I let go of all that *fear* ... and started to just enjoy myself a little—well, things weren't nearly as bad as I always thought they'd be. *(Beat.)* Take it from one who *knows,* Brian. All your fears are groundless.

STATE OF MIND

I always thought, once I moved out here into the middle of nowhere, that I'd be a better person. You know, once I got away from the whole subway thing. The commuting thing. The office thing. The pressure thing. The deadline thing. The dating thing. The not-enough-hours-in-a-day thing. Once I got away from all those things and got out here where I could have some peace and quiet and fresh air—*(Takes a deep breath of air, then exhales.)*—that I would *relax*. *(Beat.)* Well, it doesn't work that way. You see, Diane, I've come to believe that there are two kinds of people in this world: relaxers and nail-biters. Now you know me, ever since Grade School at P.S. 115 I've been a real nail-biter. Nervous and antsy all the time. Jumpy. The doorbell rings, I jump. A dog barks, I jump. My mother coughs at the other end of the house—I jump! It's no good. But I thought, once I got out *here*, away from the constant stress of the city, that I would finally *relax*. *(Beat.)* You think so? Look. *(Holds up her hands to show her nails.)* They're just as chewed-up as before! I don't know what the trouble is, I've shunned everything I can think of that made me nervous. I've bought myself an entire new set of surroundings! A whole new life! And *still* I can't seem to relax! *(Beat.)* The minister down at our church says it's all a state of mind. I told him, I said, "I changed states already but I *still* got the same mind." He laughed. But I don't really believe he thought it was funny. *(Beat.)* *You're* always calm, Diane. You always seem like you're on top of things. How do *you* do it?—And *don't* tell me it's a state of mind. I need something I can sink my *teeth* into.

STRENGTH

All my life, crises have seemed to bring out the *worst* in me. A problem presents itself, I fold up like a card table. That's always been the pattern. When Mom died, I locked myself in the house for a whole *month*. You remember that? The Fire Department finally had to break in and drag me out. I hadn't eaten for weeks—oh, it was awful. All sorts of things like that, along the way. I flunked out of college, I folded up. Steven—(*Beat.*)—he broke off our engagement ... and I folded up. God knows where he is now. And when they told me this yesterday! My first thought—the first thing that came rushing into my mind—was, "You can always kill yourself." And I thought, of course! That's the easiest solution! So I started trying to figure out the best way. Should I take a bunch of pills? Shoot myself? What's fast and not messy? So there I am pondering all those ideas and just when I was about to fold ... at that point of no return ... something stopped me. Some ... force—I don't know exactly what, call it a divine presence if you want—but something suddenly gave me *strength*. Maybe it was the realization that now I'm living for *two people*. That I had to be strong for two people now, not just one. (*Beat.*) I am going to have this baby, Jennifer. This is the strength I've been looking for all my life. And I will nurture it until it shines as bright as the sun. So don't cry, Jennifer. *I'm* not. I think from now on ... crises will bring out the *best* in me.

SWIMMING WITH SHARKS

I used to want to save the world. Then I got a little weary of trying to do that and decided I just wanted to make it a better place. And now, all I want to do is just survive. I went back to my high school reunion and everybody was the same way. You could tell they were trying to put something over, trying to act like they were such big shots, so successful and everything, but you could tell they were all struggling to survive, just like me. You could see it in their eyes. Their eyes were dead. (*Beat.*) Why is everything so hard? Why does it take every ounce of strength I've got just to get through a day? My friend Kim, she's really into vitamins. She takes about fifteen or twenty vitamin pills a day. And *shots* ... her butt looks like a pin cushion. She claims these vitamins give her "extra endurance." Allow her to rise above the rest of the "struggling masses," as she calls us. But I just think they've made her a nervous wreck. She chatters endlessly without waiting for you to answer and chews her fingernails to the quick. Makes me so jumpy! When we're kids, everything seems so easy. Our parents shelter us and take care of us and lead us to believe that we're never going to have to *worry* about anything when we go out into the World. And then we get out into the world and it's like ... it's like swimming with sharks! (*Beat.*) I wish I could help you, Belinda. I really, really wish I could. But this time, you're gonna have to save the world without me. I gotta worry about saving my*self* first.

THE $10,000 WOMAN

You like my butt? This is a *new* butt. I got tired of my *old* butt ...
so I bought a *new* one. (*Gestures to it.*) $1,600. And these—(*Her
breasts.*)—$1,200. And my cheeks, my nose, and my chin. I'm the
$10,000 woman! It meant about a zillion hours of overtime, but it
was *worth* it! Don't you think? I think so. Because *now* ... when I
walk into a party ... every guy's head turns. They *study* my butt!
Nobody *used* to study my butt. But now they do. I could've
exercised for the next three hundred years and never had a butt like
this! Look. (*SHE models.*) All you have to do is just sign up for a
bunch of extra shifts ... save up your money ... and go get a new
butt. Trust me, Helen. Your life will change ... (*Strikes a pose.*) ...
DRAMATICALLY!

TWO-FACED

You are so *two*-faced! You are! You are *so* two-faced. You are so two-faced that you make me want to *vomit*! I'm serious! Stick my finger right down my throat and—(*Demonstrates, making a barfing sound.*)—vomit! (*Beat.*) I never realized that our office was so full of cliques. And I never realized that you were part of *every one of them*! Oh, no? When you're around Barry and Fred, all of a sudden you're this big sports fan. The three of you just sit around all day, ridiculing people like me who couldn't dribble a ball if their *life* depended on it. And then, when you're around Janet and Melba! All of a sudden, you're such a "radical," you all just rag on people like me, who dress a little preppie. And when you're around *me*, you rag on ALL OF THEM! It's sickening. It really is downright sickening. How can you stand to sit there and ridicule *everybody*? It's like, your whole life is based on GOSSIP! (*Beat.*) I don't want to be part of your cliques. You got that? I don't want to sit around and *judge* everybody else in this office because I am sick and tired of watching *you* do it. I—(*Beat.*) What? She did *what*? That bitch! I never liked her. (*Leans in, conspiratorially.*) You know what *I* heard ... ?

UH-HUH

Uh-huh. Uh-huh. Yeah, I—(*Beat.*) Uh-huh. (*Beat.*) Sure, uh-huh. I
know what you—uh-huh. (*Beat.*) Wow. Yeah. Listen—what? Oh,
yeah. Uh-huh. Listen, could you—huh? (*Beat.*) Oh. You did, eh?
That's really—that's really fascinating, but—(*Beat.*) Uh-huh. Uh-
huh. Hey, look, it's getting kind of late, and—Uh-huh. Uh-huh,
well, I—JESUS CHRIST, ARE YOU GOING TO KEEP
SPOUTING FORTH ALL NIGHT LONG? YOU'RE WORSE
THAN MOUNT VESUVIUS, SOME ERUPTING VOLCANO!
DO I GET ONE FUCKING WORD IN EDGEWISE? OR IS THAT
TOO MUCH TO ASK! God, I *swear* ... Listen, Raymond. You're
not a bad guy, okay? You were really nice when you first picked me
up tonight. Held the car door open for me ... brought me flowers ...
when was the last time somebody brought me flowers? The thing is
... you just *talk* too much. I told Sherry I'd go out with you; she
said blind date and these red flags went up inside my head, you
know, but you sounded nice so I said "Okay, I'll go." You sounded
lonely. Is it any wonder? You must DRIVE people away from you
with—with YOUR TORRENT OF WORDS! We have been sitting
here since eight-thirty. We haven't ordered yet, because you wanted
to get through your "life story" first. Fine. I'm all for familiarity.
But it's ELEVEN NINETEEN and my STOMACH IS CLOSING
IN ON ITSELF! What, was I supposed to staple it together before I
came here tonight? I swear I am going to faint from hunger if we
don't order soon and I am going to go INSANE IF YOU DON'T
STOP TALKING, TALKING, TALKING, TALKING,
TALKING!!!! (*Pause.*) Uh-huh. Uh-huh. Yeah, well—(*Beat.*) Uh-
huh. Uh-huh ... Listen, Raymond—(*Beat; SHE's just too weary to
fight.*) Never mind.

109

WALKING COOKBOOK

You know a *lot* about food, don't you, Martin? You're a regular Galloping Gourmet. (*Beat.*) I'm not making fun. I'm *serious*! You're a regular walking cookbook! *Every* time we sit down to eat, I am so privileged to hear your dissertation on where the dish originated: the country, the century. You're always considerate enough to point out how the dish set before us was *in*correctly prepared. Not to your liking. Mmmm. (*Big, warm smile.*) I'm so lucky. Any girl would be jealous of me. To share the experiences we share. Like at that lovely little Italian restaurant last night! How *lucky* I was to be there when you told the waiter—in excruciating detail—how the calamari *should* have been prepared. "Sauteed first, *then* fried. And fried lightly. Not burned to a crisp." Oh, how *wonderful* it was to watch you go back into the kitchen and berate the chef! How *heroic*! I'll bet you think it's impressive to watch you behave like that. I'll bet you think it's *sexy*. I'll bet you think I *love* to hear you criticize *my* cooking too. That I love to hear you bitch about every dish I've ever cooked for you. How you critique the bechamel sauce on my crepes ... the basting of my turkey ... the creme in my *eclairs*!—While I watch you stuff each forkful of food into your mouth! (*Beat.*) You think I like all that, Martin? Well, I've got news for you: it *sucks*! It really and truly *sucks*! (*Smiles.*) But I don't mind. I don't, really. And I'm *so* glad to hear that you enjoyed my liver pate. I'm so glad to know that it was prepared "properly," just like "Madame LeRonde herself would have done at the cooking school in Paris." You *really* have taught me so much about food, Martin. I hope I'm going to teach you something too ... So listen carefully, Martin, because I'm only going to say this *once*: that delicious pate you just licked off your fingertips? It was CAT FOOD. (*Beat; SHE rises.*) Goodbye, Martin. It's been nice cooking for you.

WELL INFORMED

I have come to depend more and more on television. In a busy world like ours, how could you *not*? I mean, who has time to sit and read the paper anymore? You watch a news update and you get all the world news in two or three minutes. And *entertainment* too! Why go out and spend all that money on plays or movies when you've got hundreds of channels to choose from? I own five TV's: one in the bedroom, one in the bathroom, and three in the living room—one for each of the major networks. So I am *constantly* in touch with the outside world. There is nothing that doesn't happen—that is televised—that escapes my notice. I used to have a job, but now I work at home. Stuffing envelopes ... telemarketing ... anything to keep me near the glow of my picture tubes. My Ma thinks I'm really crazy cause I never go *out* anymore. She says to me, she says, "Aren't you lonely?" Sure, I *guess* I get a little lonely sometimes, who doesn't? But that's the price you pay for being well informed. Besides, I told her, "Why bother going out?" As long as I can call for them to deliver Chinese, why should I? In fact, I'm so close to the Hwangs now that they'll even bring me my *groceries*! The only reason I came out tonight was for some fresh milk. And of course I got to meet *you*! So what do you say, Darryl? I know you like me. I can see it in your eyes. You want to come up and watch television? (*A sly laugh, menacing in a way.*) I *may* never let you leave!

WHAT IF

People think I'm such an angel ... but if they only knew what was *really* going on inside my head, they'd *shudder*! Yesterday, I sat there for two hours while we had that nauseatingly monotonous Board Meeting. And all I could think was, "What would happen if I just crawled across the table and chewed Marshall's *face* off?" Not that I have any enmity against Marshall. He's a perfectly fine guy to work for. And not that I would even really do anything—well, *cannibalistic*. But what would they all *do* if I just ... ripped his nose off with my teeth and then spit it out on the table in front of them? Something just really, really *weird*? (*Beat.*) "What if" is a question that haunts me. "What if" I ran over somebody with the Volkswagen? "What if" I spray-painted obscene words across the windows of the Safeway? "What if" I took all my clothes off and stood, start naked, in the middle of Chestnut Street and GAVE AWAY MY RECORD COLLECTION? (*Beat.*) This is probably a sign of something. That I have some ... imbalance somewhere. Or something. Or maybe modern life is just so *dull* that we have to fantasize. You know, maybe daydreaming is healthy. What I'm trying to say is, the next time we have a Board Meeting ... if you see me sit up and start to do something *stupid*—STOP ME. Will you? Before it's too late.